Blocks and Quilts Everywhere!

by Debbie Caffrey

Dedication

To all who make quilts to warm the hearts and bodies of those they love.

Acknowledgements

There are many people not mentioned here who have inspired and encouraged me to produce this book. I want to extend a sincere thanks to all of you, the participants in my "Sample These" workshops.

Many thanks are sent to these wonderful people, too:

Thanks go to Jo Ann Gruber for the use of her quilt, *Sew Many Treasured Memories*. Jo Ann's talent created one of the most interesting settings in the book.

I greatly appreciate the professionalism and quality of work that I received from those involved in the production of this book, especially my photographer and everyone at the printing company. They worked very well within the tight deadlines that I set.

I would have been lost without my children Monica, Erin, and Mark. They spent hours proofreading. In addition, Erin kept the rest of business running smoothly to allow me time for writing.

Finally, and very importantly, my husband Dan is responsible for helping me keep things in perspective. At least he *tried*. Right in the middle of writing this book, he took me to Scotland where we spent twelve glorious, sunny days celebrating our twenty-fifth anniversary.

Credits

Photographer

Mark Frey
P.O. Box 1596
Yelm, WA 98597

Printer

Professional Colorgraphics
5611 Silverado Way, Suite D
Anchorage, AK 99518

Blocks and Quilts Everywhere!
©1997 by Debbie Caffrey

ISBN   0-9645777-1-2

Published by
Debbie's Creative Moments
4801 Jumar Avenue
Anchorage, AK 99516
USA

All rights reserved. No part of this book may be reproduced in any manner without written permission from the publisher.

I encourage the use of this book as a basis for classes, provided that each student is required to purchase a copy.

These patterns are to be used to produce quilts for personal use. There should be no commercial production of these quilts without written permission. Respect all copyright laws. When in doubt, ask the author or publisher.

Front cover quilt:

On the Trail, 43" x 55".

This quilt was designed as a mystery quilt to debut in a class at Quilt Festival 1997 in Houston, Texas. Its complete name is *On the Trail to Festival.*

Table of Contents

Introduction	**4**
Chapter 1 - General Instructions	**5**
Chapter 2 - Fabric Selection	**12**
Photo Gallery	**17**
Chapter 3 - Quilt Construction	
Step in Time	**25**
On the Trail	**27**
Homesteader's Daughters	**30**
Tuesday's Child	**33**
Snips & Snails	**34**
Who Has the Old Maid?	**36**
Sew Many Treasured Memories	**39**
Ginger Snaps	**41**
Gemstones	**43**
Q-Bert	**47**
Chapter 4 - Block Construction	
Block Patterns	**50**
Line Drawings	**83**
Index	**87**
Conversion Charts	**88**

Introduction

The six inch blocks in this book are like potato chips. It is impossible to stop after just one! Almost as soon as you begin the block it is finished, leaving you anxious to make another.

Whenever you have the time, perhaps on a weekend, spend a day selecting fabrics, cutting pieces, and placing them on a design wall. You will want to sew, but keep cutting. This allows you to make changes in some of the earlier blocks as you see them next to others. These changes are much easier to make before the blocks are sewn. When you have finished cutting, put the remaining fabrics into a neat stack, clean up the sewing area, and relax.

Later, during the work week, piece the blocks. Piecing takes an average of fifteen minutes each! Sew a block while you wait for a pot of water to boil, make another while the dryer finishes, and piece two more after you put the kids to bed. By the end of the week you will have twenty blocks pieced. And you thought there was no time to quilt.

I hope you will use this book to create your own quilts. Mix and match the design elements presented. The following ideas are just to get your thoughts in motion.

Try using the Snail's Trail setting shown on the front cover with sampler blocks.

Make *Q-Bert* with different colors of sashing on each block to really give the illusion of a stack of children's building blocks.

Use setting blocks and sashing like those in *Gemstones*, but set the blocks squarely instead of on point.

Consider what *Step in Time* would look like if it was set on point.

Have fun making your quilts with a little help from this book. I'd love to see the results!

Chapter 1

General Instructions

It is very important to take the time to review this chapter prior to using the block and quilt patterns. Many of the questions that can arise by going directly to the construction chapters will be answered here.

The blocks in Chapter 4 are 6" square when finished. They should measure 6 1/2" with their seam allowances. All of the quilt patterns in this book use the 6" blocks. On page 88 there are four conversion charts. These enable you to make any of the eighty blocks into a 12" block for use in other quilts you design.

Fabric Preparation

The fabric *yardage requirements* in this book are generous. They allow for shrinkage, straightening, and minor goofs. Most fabrics are not 44" wide. If your fabrics have at least 40" of usable width (Beware of those wide selvages!), you will have enough unless otherwise noted.

I prefer to wash fabrics to remove the sizing and excess dye prior to cutting. Wash colors separately using whatever soap you plan to use for your quilt. There are specialty soaps available at quilt shops should you choose to use them. Do not overload the dryer or over dry your fabrics.

To avoid distorting your fabric as you press the yardage, move your iron in strokes that are parallel to the selvages. This is in the direction of the stable warp yarns which do not stretch with the iron's strokes. Too often I have had quilters come to class with fabrics that seem to have wavy, wobbly edges along the selvages. Most of the time this problem is not due the quality of the fabric. It is created by moving the iron from side to side between the selvages, while applying any combination of the following: heavy pressure on the iron, a lot of steam, and starch or sizing.

Cutting

These blocks and quilts have been designed for *rotary cutting*. No templates are provided. Most of you are quite familiar with your rotary cutter. With that in mind, I have elected to use this section to clarify my cutting instructions, and offer suggested techniques that will build upon your basic skills. If you do not already know how to use a rotary cutter, you will find a section in every issue of almost any quilting magazine on the market that describes rotary cutting. Take an introductory lesson or attend a demonstration at your local quilt shop. A great reference book for teaching yourself rotary cutting basics is *Measure the Possibilities with Omnigrid*, by Nancy Johnson-Srebro.

When the instructions refer to *cutting strips, the strips are cut across the width of the fabric*, making them approximately 42" long with selvages on each of the short ends. The exception to this is when cutting strips for borders, which will be explained in the border section of this chapter.

Every piece you will cut is a square, rectangle, half-square triangle, or quarter-square triangle. Generally, squares and rectangles are cut so that the outside edges are on the straight of grain (lengthwise and crosswise grains). You may choose to "fussy cut" or otherwise cut your pieces off grain to take advantage of the fabric's print. This may result in bias edges along the outside edges of the blocks. Careful handling of these pieces can avoid distorting the finished block. Use spray starch or sizing on these fabrics, prior to cutting, to stabilize them.

Half-square and quarter-square triangles are the same shape, but their difference is very important to quilting. Both triangles have two short sides of equal length, one right angle (a 90 degree corner), and two 45 degree corners. The difference is where their bias and on grain edges appear.

Half-square triangles have two short sides on the straight of grain and the long side on the bias. Half-square triangles are used for a block like the Pinwheel.

Quarter-square triangles have two short

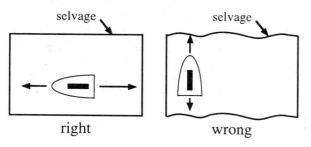

5

sides on the bias and the long side on the straight of grain. These are the triangles that are used for a block like Big Dipper. Many blocks, like Pinwheel on Point, use triangles of each kind.

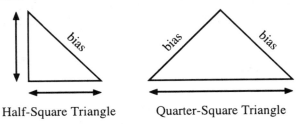

 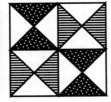 
Pinwheel   Big Dipper   Pinwheel on Point

The patterns in Chapters 3 and 4 give you specific cutting instructions for the half-square and quarter-square triangles. In addition to the written instructions, you are reminded of how to cut them by a little sketch like those shown below.

Half-Square Triangle   Quarter-Square Triangle

I have made great friends with the Omnigrid 96 triangle tool, shown below. There is a larger version, the 96L, which works as well. These are *tools*, not rulers. The seam allowances are built into the size markings. The 96's are used for cutting half-square triangles. Do not confuse them with the Omnigrid 98's, which are used for cutting quarter-square triangles. I don't use the 98 very often, but I find the 96 is always on my cutting table.

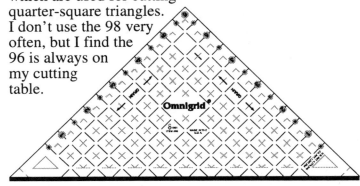

Detailed instructions for using this tool are in the book, *Measure the Possibilities with Omnigrid*, which was recommended earlier. For an example of how the Omnigrid 96 is used, see below.

Example:
Assume that you are cutting the pieces for a Shoo-Fly block. When using scraps, cutting two different sizes of squares does not affect your leftover fabric very much.

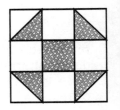

If you are using yardage, though, instead of making "Swiss cheese" of the fabric while cutting different sizes, all of the required pieces can be cut from a 2 1/2" strip of light fabric and a 2 1/2" strip of dark fabric.

Cutting the 2 1/2" square is obvious. To cut the half-square triangles, align the size 2 line with the bottom edge of the 2 1/2" strip, putting a short side of the triangle even with the squared end of the strip. See below. (Remember, seam allowances are built in. Use the finished size.) The tip of the triangle will hang over the top edge of the strip by 3/8", right where the short dashed line appears. Cut along the diagonal. The resulting triangle will have one pointed corner and one blunt corner. Don't worry, the missing pointed tip is excess seam allowance, a "dog ear", that will need to be trimmed during construction anyway.

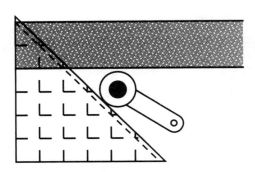

Now, rotate the tool a half turn, align the size 2 line at the top of the strip and the long diagonal edge of the triangle with the freshly cut angle of the strip. Again, the tip of the tool will extend 3/8" beyond the edge of the strip. Cut the second triangle. Repeat these instructions to cut as many triangles as you need for the block.

6

Piecing

A ***precise seam allowance*** is the key to a successful quilt. Use scant 1/4" seam allowances, unless directed to do otherwise. A scant 1/4" seam allowance is a needle's width narrower than a true 1/4". It's a small difference, but necessary to accommodate for the fabric that is taken up in the "roll" when seam allowances are pressed to the side. It would be a good idea to do the following test to check your seam allowances.

Test:

Cut four 1 1/2" x 4 1/2" rectangles. Sew them together along the long sides, as shown in the sketch at the right. Press the seam allowances to one side. Measure the piece.

It should measure 4 1/2" x 4 1/2". If not, adjust your seam allowance and repeat the test until you find the correct seam allowance. Take advantage of the options available on your machine. You may be able to move your needle to the left or right to make slight adjustments, or perhaps, use a different presser foot. Taking the time to establish an accurate seam allowance will save you hours of frustration in the future.

Use twelve stitches per inch (2.0).

Sew with right sides together. **RST** is the abbreviation used throughout the instructions.

Chain piece whenever possible. Feed your pieces through the machine without breaking the thread between them. It not only saves time and thread, but makes piecing more precise. Also, with the stitching anchored in the previous pieces, you will not have your machine "eating the corners" of the next pieces as you begin sewing them.

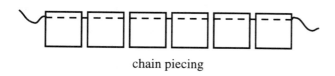

chain piecing

Change your needle often. Do not wait for one to break. Use a size 12/80. Specialty needles are made for specific uses, such as quilting with metallic threads. Depending upon the size of your quilts and how much machine quilting you have done, you may need to change your needle after one to three quilts.

The sketches in Chapters 3 and 4 show the blocks, units, and sections as they look when they are finished. There are no seam allowances shown on them. Because of their small sizes, showing the seam allowances would be more confusing than helpful. Here I will elaborate on piecing a few specific shapes. The seam allowances are shown in these larger sketches.

Assuming that they are cut correctly, squares and rectangles align perfectly at each end of the seam line. That's not the case when sewing triangles to squares or half-square triangles to quarter-square triangles.

Sewing triangles to squares :

Follow the instructions directly below to make pieced triangular units like the one at the right. Keep these instructions in mind when sewing your diagonal rows for quilts that are set on point.

Start by aligning the square corners of the square and first triangle. The point of the triangle will extend beyond the other end of the square by ***3/8"***, not just a 1/4", as you might expect. See the sketch below. This is necessary in order to create enough allowance for the next seam. After stitching the first seam, press the seam allowances toward the triangle. Trim the "dog ear", as shown by the solid line. A ***dog ear*** is that little triangular tab of fabric in the seam allowance that extends beyond the edges of the unit. Trim these away as they occur. They will only cause bulk and make it difficult to match the seam lines.

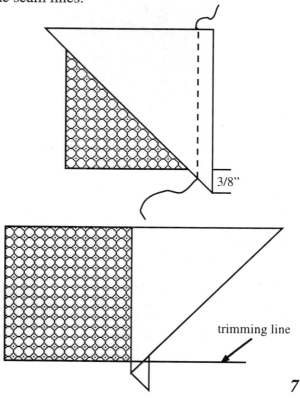

7

Now, align the second triangle on the adjacent side of the unit. Notice how the two angles of the pieces meet exactly at the seam line. Stitch. Press the seam allowances toward the triangle that you just added. Trim the dog ears. You will have a 1/4" seam allowance between the corner of the square and raw edge of the pieced unit.

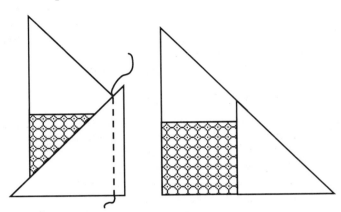

If you are making a unit like the one at the right, the points of the first triangle will extend 3/8" beyond the square on both ends of the seam line. See the sketch below.

Stitch, press the seam allowances toward the triangle, and trim the dog ears.

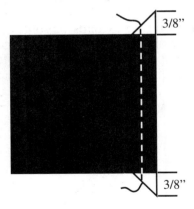

Repeat the above step, adding a triangle to the opposite side of the square.

Finally, add triangles to the remaining two sides of the square. When adding these triangles, the two angles of the pieces will meet exactly at the seam line on both ends. Stitch. Press the seam allowances toward the triangles and trim the dog ears.

At this point, there will be a 1/4" seam allowance between the corners of the inner square and the edges of the unit on all four sides.

Sewing triangles to each other:

Sewing triangles together can be challenging, too. For example, consider making the Flying Geese unit shown at the right.

Align 45 degree angles of the triangles at the top end of the seam line. The other 45 degree angle of the half-square triangle will extend beyond the square corner of the quarter-square triangle by 3/8". Stitch and press the seam allowances toward the smaller triangle. Trim the dog ears.

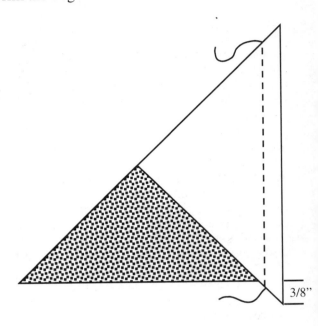

Add the second half-square triangle to the other short side of the quarter-square triangle to complete the unit. This time the 45 degree angles will match at the corner of the unit, and the two angles of the opposite end (at the top of the unit) will meet at the seam line. Stitch. Press the seam allowances toward the triangle you just added. Trim the dog ears.

At this point, there will be a 1/4" seam allowance between the square corner of the large triangle and the top edge of the unit.

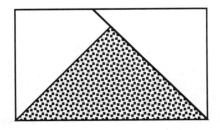

Sew & flip technique:

Some sections of the blocks in this book contain trapezoids. Instead of using templates, they are accomplished with a sew & flip technique.

Start by placing a square, RST, on one end of the rectangle. Stitch on the diagonal of the square from corner to corner, as shown by the dotted line. It is very important that you stitch in direction shown for each block. Otherwise, you may end up with pieces that are the reverses of those you need! Check your work before trimming. Trim away the excess as shown by the solid line in the sketch. Press the seam allowances to one side.

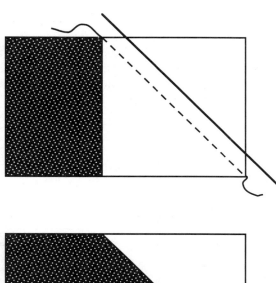

More piecing tips:

If you find that your piecing has been a little less than perfectly precise, you may need to make some adjustments. It is a rare occasion that I do any trimming or suggest it as a solution to quilters in my workshops. Trimming can really create problems later down the line. It's a good way to have flat tips on your triangles.

Instead of trimming, match the seam lines and pin in place. Ease any difference in size between the pins. If one or both of the pieces that you are trying to ease together will not stretch, sewing with the larger piece on the bottom will allow the feed dogs of your sewing machine to gradually work in the fullness.

Even when the blocks are finished I don't trim and square them. If the quilt uses sashing or alternate setting squares of fabric, determine what size to cut them by finding an average size of your pieced blocks. Cutting the sashes and squares to custom fit your blocks will make assembling the quilt much easier, and the finished project will look better.

Examples:

If your blocks range in size from 6" to 6 1/2", cut your sashing strips 6 1/4" long. On the other hand, if most of your blocks measure 6 1/2" and just a couple of them are 6", cut your sashing strips 6 1/2" long.

Pressing

Pressing is a very important part of accurately pieced blocks. Take care not to distort your blocks by moving your iron over the pieces while applying too much pressure. The weight of your iron alone should be enough pressure. I use a steam iron.

First, set your seams by pressing the stitches flat. Then press the seam allowances from the right side to avoid creating a pleat at the seam line.

There are specific directions for pressing throughout the patterns. I press in the direction which is best for the construction of the blocks and quilts. That includes pressing the seam allowances open, at times, and not always pressing the seam allowances toward the dark fabric. There are arrows in many of the sketches showing my suggested pressing directions.

Arrows that have points on both ends suggest that you press those seam allowances open. I press seam allowances open when making pieces like the sawtooth section below. With the seam allowances pressed open you are able to see the points of the triangles on both sides of the section as you sew it into the quilt. This way you will avoid flattening any of the tips. Pressing these seam allowances open eliminates very bulky areas, too.

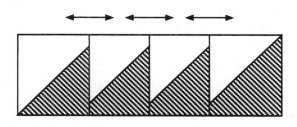

9

Borders

Five of the quilts in this book have borders added to them. Whenever possible, the **outer border strips should be cut with the lengthwise grain in the long direction.** This will keep them from stretching and rippling. *Sew Many Treasured Memories* has three narrow borders before the outer wide border. It is not necessary that the inner borders be cut along the lengthwise grain.

Measuring and easing are important steps. Without them your quilt may be different lengths on opposite sides and will not be square. Be sure the quilt is pressed well before measuring. As you are measuring, keep the quilt top fairly taut on a flat surface. (Do not stretch the quilts that are set on point.) Measuring otherwise could result in borders that are too short. The quilt top contains many seams, and they each have a slight amount of slack where the seam allowances are pressed to the side. Conversely, the borders have few or no seams and are cut along the stable, lengthwise grain.

Borders can be applied with either overlapped or mitered corners. Those with overlapped corners are simpler.

Overlapped corners:

Find the length of the quilt. Measure in several places (along seam lines and in areas that go through the center of the blocks, but not along the outside edges) to determine the average length. Cut two border strips 1" wider than the desired finished width by the length of the quilt. Pin them to the sides of the quilt, matching the center points and ends of the quilt and borders. Continue pinning the borders to the quilt easing, if necessary. Sew. Press the seam allowances toward the borders.

Now, determine the width of the quilt, measuring in several places, as before. Include the additional width created by the side borders. Cut two border strips to fit (finished border width plus 1" x width of quilt) and pin them to the top and bottom of the quilt as you did the side borders. Sew. Press the seam allowances toward the borders.

If you are adding more than one border, repeat the above steps for each one.

quilt with overlapped borders

Mitered corners:

Determine both the width and length of your quilt. Allow extra length to all of the borders as you cut them. Add two times the border width plus an inch or two to the measurements of your quilt. If the quilt will have more than one border with mitered corners, sew the borders together into a panel before attaching them. See page 40.

Even with mitered corners you can square your quilt. Put a pin at the center of each border. Measure half the length of your quilt in each direction from the center of the border and mark these points with pins. Now, pin the border to your quilt, matching the pins with the center and ends of the quilt. Use additional pins as needed.

Attach borders to two opposite sides of the quilt, first. **Begin and end the stitching on the seam line, 1/4" from the edge of the quilt top.** Backstitch at both ends. Press the seam allowances toward the borders. Repeat with the remaining two border pieces.

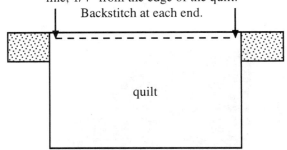

Place a corner of the quilt on the ironing board. See below. Lay the vertical border on the ironing board first. Lay the horizontal border over it, as shown.

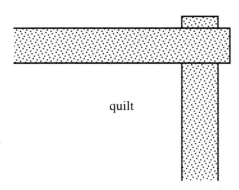

10

Tuck the end of the top border under so that the fold makes a 45 degree angle. Press. Lay a rotary cutting ruler on top of this corner to check that it is square and the angle is accurate. If your border is strip pieced, make sure the seam lines match.

Place the borders, RST, and pin. Match seam lines, if necessary. Stitch on the pressed crease, starting on the seam line, being careful not to catch the quilt top in the stitching. Stitch to the outer edge of the border. Check your work. Make sure you are pleased with the finished corner before doing any trimming. If it is correct, trim the excess fabric, leaving 1/4" for seam allowances. Press the seam allowances to one side or open.

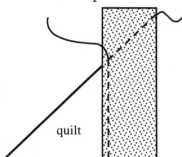

Place the borders RST, and stitch on the pressed crease, starting on the seam line, and being careful not to catch the quilt top in the stitching.

Quilting and Binding

These two skills are like rotary cutting. They are basic skills that have books and classes dedicated solely to them. Again, almost every quilting magazine on the market contains basic instruction for quilting and binding in every issue. Take advantage of demonstrations and classes that are available to you. The quilting and binding on quilts are highly visible and are a part of every quilt. Learn to do them well.

All of the quilts in this book were machine quilted on regular sewing machines. Jo Ann Gruber quilted hers with metallic thread. I quilted all of mine with nylon thread, using clear for the lighter quilts and smoke-colored for the darker quilts.

Batting

Consult the information on or in the package to determine if the batting is suitable for the quilting method you choose, how closely it must be quilted, and preparation and washing instructions for that specific batting.

I prefer cotton batting. I used the following two battings in these quilts: the thinnest batting from Quilter's Cotton, which is about the same thickness as a heavy flannel, and Hobbs Heirloom cotton batting, a blend of 80% cotton and 20% polyester.

Binding

If you need detailed information on binding, *Happy Endings*, by Mimi Dietrich, published by That Patchwork Place, is a good reference.

After quilting, trim the excess batting and backing in preparation for binding. I use a 1/2" wide binding. Many quilts have pieced edges, and therefore, have only 1/4" seam allowances. To allow for the 1/2" binding, trim the backing and batting, leaving an additional 1/4" beyond the raw edge. This will create the necessary 1/2" seam allowance.

For a 1/2" double binding, cut crossgrain strips 3 1/4" wide. Bias strips are only necessary for binding curves, although, some fabrics, like plaids and stripes, make a more interesting binding when cut on the bias. Cut enough strips to go around the perimeter of your quilt. Sew them together, end on end, and press the seam allowances open. Press the strip, wrong sides together, lengthwise.

Sew the binding to the quilt with 1/2" seam allowances, aligning the raw edges of the binding with the cut edge of the quilt. Start in the middle of one side, leaving the first six inches of binding unsewn. Stitch, stopping 1/2" from the corner. Lift your presser foot and pull the quilt out a few inches from under the machine to fold the binding. I don't clip the threads. Rotate the quilt a quarter turn, counterclockwise. Fold the binding up and away, creating a 45 degree angle. Then, fold the binding back down toward you.

Begin stitching at the edge of the quilt. Continue stitching down the second side, stopping 1/2" from the corner. Miter this corner as you did the first one. After you have mitered the last corner, stop stitching 12" from where you first began to attach the binding.

Trim the excess binding, leaving 1/2" extra for seam allowances. Stitch the two ends of the binding together with a 1/4" seam allowance. Press the seam allowances open. Finish stitching this section of the binding to the quilt.

Push the binding to the back of the quilt and pin in place. Fold the corners into neat miters on the back of the quilt. The folded edge of the binding should cover the stitching line. Hand stitch the binding into place.

Sign, date, and enjoy your quilt!

Chapter 2
Fabric Selection

How many times have you heard someone say, *"I'm just not good with color!"*? Maybe you've said this yourself. When I hear this my first thought is, I'll bet she can name the colors in the rainbow, and she would know how to mix paints in the primary colors to make orange, green, or purple. This is what color is. It's just that simple.

Now, I didn't say that fabric selection was that basic! Let me present a few concepts to consider.

Color

You know the concept of a color wheel, primary colors, and the colors that are created when two primary colors are combined. All that's missing may be the confidence and skill to employ this knowledge.

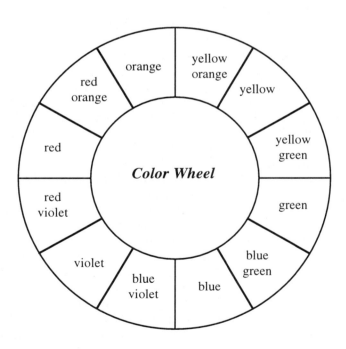

Most anything goes with color combinations. Color schemes may be **monochrome**, **analogous**, **complimentary**, or a combination. It is not necessary that you concern yourself with the technical terms, just learn the basic ideas behind them.

Monochrome

Monochrome simply means one color.

Analogous

An analogous color scheme is one that uses colors that are next to each other on the color wheel, such as, blue, blue-violet, and violet. *Gemstones* is an example of an analogous color scheme that pushes the range to include additional colors on each end (green through red-violet). When using this color scheme, try not to have a big jump between two colors and very little between the next two, as you move around the color wheel. This is not an easy task when you are working with fabrics. That's where having a great fabric stash and access to a wonderful quilt shop come in handy.

Complimentary

Colors that are across from each other on the color wheel develop a complimentary color scheme. Examples are: red and green; violet and yellow; and red-violet and yellow-green.

Contrast is an important term to know. Contrast between two colors can be described by how far apart they are on the color wheel. Complimentary colors, since they are across the wheel from each other, have the highest contrast between them. Colors next to each other are said to have low contrast. Fabrics can contrast in value, also. That is discussed later in the section on value.

Triad

This is my term for three colors that are equidistant from each other on the color wheel. The most obvious example of what I mean is a primary color scheme; red, yellow, and blue. Look at *Snips and Snails* on page 24. The main color scheme for this quilt is a triad: yellow-green, blue-violet, and red-orange.

The color information presented above is just a starting place. Believe it or not, color is not very important to successful fabric selection. As I said earlier, anything you like is a good color combination. What makes fabric selection for a quilt successful is covered in the rest of this chapter.

Intensity

Intensity refers to the pureness and clarity of the color. Intense colors are like those found in a box of eight crayons. A fabric that has less intensity is one that might be called "dusty", such as, sage green, mauve, and colonial blue. Sometimes all that a fabric grouping needs is to replace a fabric with one that is not a different color, but more or less intense than the one currently being considered.

Value

The value of your fabrics is the most important single element in fabric selection! Value is simply how light or dark the fabric is. It has nothing to do with color or intensity. *Contrast* in value means the difference between how light and how dark fabrics are *relative* to each other. Imagine a scale of zero to one hundred with white being at zero and black being at one hundred. All other values fall somewhere between them. Different values of color have interesting names. For instance, we don't often refer to colors as light or dark orange. Instead, they are peach or rust, respectively.

A high contrast collection of fabrics will include fabrics near both ends of the scale. A low contrast collection of fabrics will have a smaller range of values.

Since value is relative, the darkest fabric of a light quilt could be lighter than the lightest fabric in a dark quilt. Therefore, when a pattern asks you to select a light and a dark fabric, they do not have to be white and black. The yellows and periwinkles of *Step in Time* on page 23 are light to medium values, but the pattern calls them lights and darks just to remind you that there needs to be contrast. The amount of contrast is your decision.

When determining the value of a print fabric, don't just look at the background. The fact that a print is on a black background does not automatically make it the darkest fabric in your grouping.

Some suggestions for determining value:

View your fabrics from a distance. Put them on a design wall and stand back, or place them at the bottom of a staircase, and view them from the top.

Make a Xerox copy of the actual fabrics. The black and white image removes the confusion of color and lets you focus on only the value.

Squint or remove your glasses. This may blur the pattern enough to read a fabric's value. Another thing you might try is looking through a camera lens, a peep hole for doors (These can be found at hardware stores, and they are easy to carry to class.), a reducing glass, or backwards through a pair of binoculars.

Visual Texture

Have you seen a fabric that looks like it should feel fuzzy or bumpy? Consider the following things when selecting fabrics for visual texture: *Scale* (size of the printed figure); *spacing* (distance between the figures); and *style* (floral, geometric, novelty print, tone on tone, etc.). Using fabrics of the same scale or spacing may cause visual confusion. Choose a variety. Consider how you will treat directional fabrics Ignore their prints or fuss with them. Be careful with your use of *solids*. The use of only one or two solid fabrics may draw too much attention to those pieces and lessen the impact of the overall design.

Proportion

The proportions of colors is important. In general, a quilt will be more interesting if the colors are not used in equal amounts. Instead, let one color be more dominant, and use the others in smaller, not necessarily equal, proportions.

Lighting

Consider the lighting when making your fabric choices, especially if you have a definite use in mind for the quilt. Will the quilt be used in an office where there is fluorescent lighting?; in a bedroom with soft lighting?; in a family room with southern exposure?; etc. Make your fabric selection in that lighting. Fabrics look much warmer in natural light. Value contrasts may need to be stronger if the lighting is lower.

Application of the Concepts

So far I have told you about what to consider when selecting fabrics. Now, I'd like to give you some "hands on" ways for using this information. Try some of the following suggestions as you pull your fabric palette together for your next quilt.

13

Safe Fabric Palettes

One almost "no fail" method of fabric selection is what I employ when designing my mystery quilt patterns. That is the idea of safe fabric palettes. Don't forget to use your basic tools - *intensity, value, visual texture, and proportion*. Once you have mastered these, push yourself to expand.

Traditional

These are tried and true combinations that are always successful: indigo and white; red and green; red, white and blue; etc.

Theme

Choose a theme for your fabrics. Examples of what I mean are: primary colors, jewel tones, seasonal (Halloween, Christmas, fall...), Victorian, tropical, plaid, etc. This list could go on forever.

Interior decorating

Decorators often use the "rule of three." They choose one floral, one geometric, and a solid or tone on tone. It is almost like "dressing your quilt." In other words, choose your fabrics like you would select clothes to wear.

Control background

I have often told quilters, "Practically any fabrics can be used together as long as you don't put them together." Part of what I mean is that if the fabrics all float on a control background fabric, it will be hard to find fabrics that you just cannot use. Old scrap quilts are great examples of this.

At the Quilt Shop

It's time to get serious and pull the fabrics for a quilt. I'll walk you through the steps like I do when helping a student select fabrics for class projects.

Probably the easiest way to approach fabric selection is with a *focus fabric*. Choose a fabric you like. This is not the time to worry about if it will work for the quilt, what other fabrics you will put with it, or anything else. Just find something that you like. Imagine that you found it, and it is a cream background with lots of green leaves and bits of lavender, gold, and pink in the flowers.

Now, analyze the fabric. Why are you attracted to it? What colors do you like in this fabric? Note the proportions, intensity, and values of the colors.

Begin *brainstorming*. Pull out fabrics that have even a remote chance of going into the quilt. **Stretch** the color, value, and intensity ranges as you gather fabrics. Ignore those cheater dots that are printed along the selvages of some fabrics. *Avoid the tendency to overmatch the colors!* Perhaps you like that print fabric we started with, but you really wish that it had peach flowers instead of pink ones. Pull peach fabrics. Set the peach fabrics next to the focus fabrics. Step back and take a look. Do the flowers now look peachy? On the other hand, if you liked the pink, but it seemed too washed out, what about using fuschia or burgundy?

Keep brainstorming! Don't make any final decisions until you've pulled dozens of fabrics. When looking at fabrics on the bolts, their proportions are almost equal. To help you imagine them in different proportions, stand them on end against a wall, layering them with the most important one, perhaps the focal print, in front. Arrange them so the fabrics that will be next to each other in the quilt are next to each other now. Expose larger amounts of fabrics that will be used often or in larger pieces and smaller amounts of those that will be used sparingly. If there are fat quarters available, use them for the small pieces in this "fabric audition". Rearrange the bolts, studying how the fabrics look when placed next to a different fabric. Look at our imaginary focus fabric. Do you think that a little gold goes a long way? If so, there is no reason to add more by using a gold fabric. Concentrate more on the green, lavender, and pink.

It's time to begin *fine tuning* your selections. It is much easier to work from many fabrics, back toward the necessary number of fabrics, than it is to work from a few and reject each new one. During the first pass, get rid of any fabric that you just don't like. Do not force it into the quilt. Are you having trouble making a decision about two or more fabrics of the same color? Why use one when many will do the job? Using several will probably add more visual texture and interest.

Select neutrals or background fabric as needed for the quilt. Audition replacement or additional fabrics. Try stretching the color range a little more or replace one or two fabrics with ones with more intensity. Remember to consider value, visual texture, proportion, etc.

As you pare down the collection of fabrics, don't be surprised if one of the fabrics that gets dismissed happens to be the original focus fabric! It has done its job by creating a wonderful fabric palette, but somehow, it no longer has a role to play in the quilt.

One of my best pieces of advice for fabric selection comes from an eighth grade English teacher. She was asked why she spent more than ten weeks teaching students to diagram sentences. After all, literary and grammatical rules are broken all the time for impact. Mrs. Finley promptly replied, "You have to know the rules in order to break them!" I have found the same in fabric selection for quilts. Knowing how and why fabrics behave as they do allows you to break the rules and design a more exciting quilt in the end.

If you have chosen a "safe" color scheme, and have gathered all of the perfect fabrics to accomplish that, you're now ready to do what Roberta Horton suggests. "Go in and mess it up a bit!" **_Have some fun and add your personality to the quilt._**

Placement of Fabrics

Look at the quilt on the back cover. It is a puzzle quilt. A puzzle quilt is a sampler which has two of each block. _Who Has the Old Maid?_ happens to have an odd one, too, just like the card game.

When making a puzzle quilt, the idea is to use color and value to create two blocks of the same pattern that look completely different from each other.

Two versions of a Big Dipper block

Using different colors for each block would make them look even less like the same block.

On page 16 there is an exercise for you to try your hand at this concept. Copy it for your personal use. Color the line drawings and try to create a block that looks different than those shown.

There are line drawings for all eighty blocks on pages 83 through 86. To see a traditional placement of values refer to the page where cutting and piecing instructions are given for that specific block (Chapter 4). You may copy pages 83 through 86 to use as coloring pages for designing your quilt.

If you choose to make a puzzle quilt, your fabric palette will need some fabrics that are close in color and value. Placing two similar fabrics next to each other in a block will suggest a different shape. I think it is cheating to sew two pieces of the same fabric together when one larger piece could have done the job.

Consider the unit below. Two quarter-square triangles of similar values have been used to create an illusion of a half-square triangle.

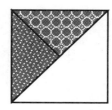

The blocks below are two different patterns, but made with the same fabrics, and, at a glance, give the illusion of being the same block.

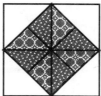 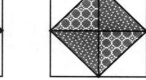

Pinwheel on Point   Broken Dishes

Now, look at the same two blocks with another fabric placement option for each.

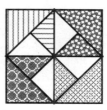 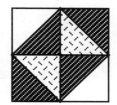

Pinwheel on Point   Broken Dishes

Why not choose your favorite block and make a quilt using only that block, but use color and value to make each block look different? Be sure the block you select has enough pieces to allow for many options. A Nine Patch block would not have enough potential, but blocks like Rabbit's Paw, Weathervane, and Country Farm are a few possibilities.

15

Tuesday's Child, *42" x 42"*

As the poem goes, "Tuesday's child is full of grace." Therefore, it is a fitting name for this quilt, which is made from the Aunt Grace's line of reproduction fabrics.

(above) **Ginger Snaps,** *34 1/2" x 43"*
What looks like a pieced border in this quilt is made very simply with
Double Four Patch blocks. One Double Four Patch is sewn onto each end of all
the rows as the quilt is assembled. It couldn't be easier!

(left) **Homesteader's Daughters,** *49" x 61"*
Alternating the Snowball and Nine Patch blocks creates a secondary pattern which is
reminiscent of the traditional Farmer's Daughter block. Since these ladies live inside
of a border made from Log Cabin blocks, I thought that they must be
the Homesteader's Daughters.

(above) *Q-Bert,* 38" x 38"

There is an electronic video game in which a little character named Q-Bert hops around from cube to cube. When my children saw this quilt, "Q-Bert" was about all they could say.

(left) **Sew Many Treasured Memories,** 63" x 71"
Designed, pieced, and machine quilted by Jo Ann Gruber, Eagle River, Alaska - 1997.

Jo Ann is a very talented quilter who created this setting for the blocks she had begun in one of the first workshops I taught based upon these six inch blocks. I had seen some of her blocks and a sketch of the setting at the last class meeting. Later, when making my quilts and preparing to write this book, I called Jo Ann to ask if I could use her quilt. She seemed a little surprised that I didn't even need to see the quilt to make the final decision. I had seen a number of her quilts, and I'm sure you'll agree, her work is beautiful!

(above) *Step in Time,* 37" x 49"

Two simple blocks set alternately give the illusion of a chorus line.
Try alternating another pair of blocks and discover the secondary pattern.

(left) *Gemstones,* 46" x 56"

Not every quilt made with 6" blocks is a little one. This one uses only twelve sampler blocks. Easy strip-pieced Linking Squares blocks, sashings, and an on point setting quickly enlarge it. Although, if you use the conversion table at the back of the book to make twelve inch blocks, you will have a twin size quilt.

Snips and Snails, 40" x 40"

I just fell in love with the frogs in the border fabric of the quilt! The blocks I used in this sampler have names that bring to mind things that little boys would appreciate. One block, Jake's Star, was named by Jo Ann Gruber to fondly remember her dog Jake (see Jo Ann's quilt, *Sew Many Treasured Memories*). Before she named the block, I thought that it looked like a tumbling toy with this fabric placement, and had planned to name it accordingly. When making a quilt for a loved one, personalize it. Choose blocks that relate to that person, or rename one that suggests another idea to you. How do you think blocks got their names in the first place, and why do many blocks have more than one name?

Chapter 3

Quilt Construction

Step in Time

Finished size is 37" x 49".

Fabric Requirements

Light #1, #2, & #3
See cutting instructions.

Light #4
1/2 yard

Dark #1, #2, & #3
See cutting instructions.

Dark #4
1/2 yard

Contrast for chain of squares
1/2 yard

Contrast for pinwheels & borders
1 3/8 yards

Backing
1 1/2 yards

Binding
1/2 yard

Cutting

Light #1
Cut one strip 2" wide.

Light #2
Cut one strip 3 1/2" wide.

Light #3
Cut one strip 5" wide.

Light #4
Cut two strips 3 7/8" wide.
    Cut these strips into seventeen 3 7/8" squares.
        Cut the squares once, diagonally, to make two half-square triangles from each.
            Yield: 34 triangles

Cut one strip 4 1/4" wide.
    Cut this strip into nine 4 1/4" squares.
        Cut the squares twice, diagonally, to make four quarter-square triangles from each.
            Yield: 36 triangles

Dark #1
Cut one strip 2" wide.

Dark #2
Cut one strip 3 1/2" wide.

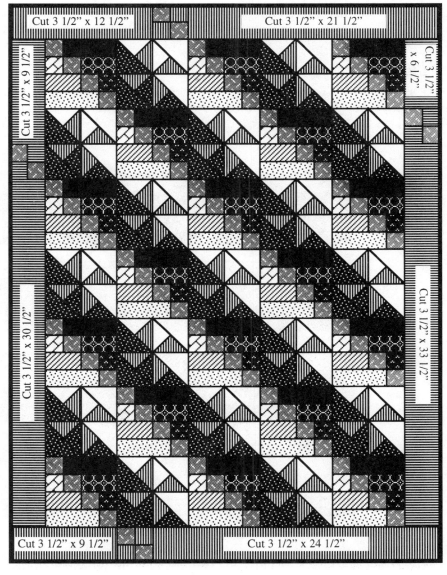

25

Dark #3
   Cut one strip 5" wide.
Dark #4
   Cut as directed for Light #4
Contrast for chain of squares
   Cut four strips 2" wide.
Contrast for pinwheels
   Cut two strips 4 1/4" wide.
      Cut these strips into seventeen 4 1/4" squares.
         Cut each square twice, diagonally, to make four quarter-square triangles from each.
            Yield: 68 triangles

Piecing

Use the strips to piece one panel of each strip combination below. Press the seam allowances toward the chain fabric. Crosscut all of the panels into eighteen sections that are 2" wide. Arrange the crosscut sections to make eighteen Up the Down Staircase blocks. Sew and press.

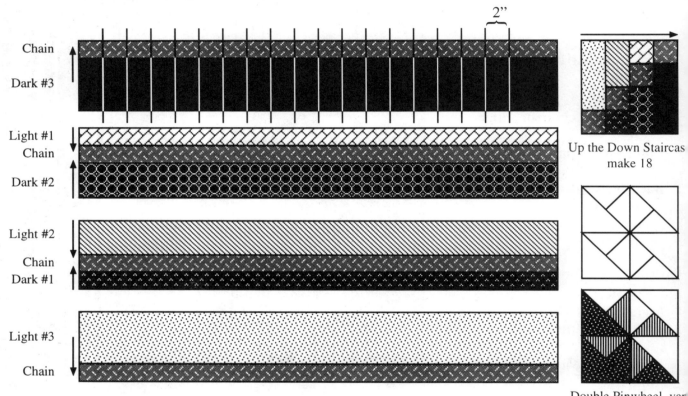

Up the Down Staircase
make 18

Double Pinwheel, var
make 17

Arrange the triangles to make seventeen Double Pinwheel variation blocks, as shown above. There will be two quarter-square triangles of Light #4 and two triangles of Dark #4 left over.
HINT: Make stacks of seventeen like pieces. Arrange the stacks to make the block. Now, chain piece to make the sewing faster and more precise.

Set the blocks into seven horizontal rows of five blocks, alternating them as shown in the graphic on the previous page. Sew them into rows. Press the seam allowances away from the Pinwheel blocks. Sew the rows together. Press.

Borders: Cut eight 2" squares of chain fabric and eight 2" squares of pinwheel fabric. Make four four patch units. Cut four 3 1/2" wide strips, lengthwise, from the remaining pinwheel fabric. Use these to cut the border pieces. The sizes are shown in the sketch on the previous page. Piece the side borders. Add them to the quilt. Press the seam allowances toward the borders. Piece the top and bottom borders. Attach them and press.

On the Trail
Finished size is 43" x 55".

Fabric Requirements

Main print
2 yards

Light
1 1/2 yards

Scraps of accent fabrics for stars
See cutting instructions.

Backing
1 3/4 yards, more if narrower than 44"

Binding
3/4 yard

Cutting

Main print
Cut three strips 2" wide.
Cut five strips 6 1/2" wide.
 Cut these strips into twenty 6 1/2" squares and fourteen 3 1/2" x 6 1/2" rectangles.
Cut three strips 3 7/8" wide.
 Cut these strips into twenty-four 3 7/8" squares.
  Cut the 3 7/8" squares once, diagonally, to make two half-square triangles from each.
  Yield: 48 triangles

Cut one strip 2 3/8" wide.
 Cut this strip into fourteen 2 3/8" squares.
  Cut the 2 3/8" squares once, diagonally, to make two half-square triangles from each.
  Yield: 28 triangles

Cut one strip 4 1/4" wide.
 Cut this strip into nine 4 1/4" squares.
  Cut the 4 1/4" squares twice, diagonally, to make four quarter-square triangles from each.
  Yield: 36 triangles

Light
Cut three strips 2" wide.
Cut three strips 2 1/2" wide.
 Cut these strips into forty-eight 2 1/2" squares.
Cut three strips 3 7/8" wide.
 Cut these strips into twenty-four 3 7/8" squares.
  Cut the 3 7/8" squares once, diagonally, to make two half-square triangles from each.
  Yield: 48 triangles

Cut two strips 2 7/8" wide.
 Cut these strips into twenty-four 2 7/8" squares.
  Cut the 2 7/8" squares once, diagonally, to make two half-square triangles from each.
  Yield: 48 triangles

Cut two strips 4 1/4" wide.
 Cut these strips into twelve 4 1/4" squares.
  Cut the 4 1/4" squares twice, diagonally, to make four quarter-square triangles from each.
  Yield: 48 triangles

On the Trail
Layout Graphic

Accent Stars

The following pieces will make one star block. You will need twelve star blocks for the quilt.

For the larger, outer star
 Cut one 2 1/2 square.
 Cut two 2 7/8" squares.
  Cut the 2 7/8" squares once, diagonally, to make two half-square triangles from each.
         Yield: 4 triangles

For the smaller, inner star
 Cut eight 1 1/2" squares.

Piecing

Use the accent star fabric pieces, the 2 1/2" squares of light fabric, and the 2 7/8" half-square triangles of light fabric to make twelve *Oh, My Stars!* blocks. Refer to page 82 for more instruction.

Sew the three 2" strips of light and main print fabrics into pairs like the one below. Press the seam allowances toward the main print. Crosscut the panels into forty-eight 2" wide sections.

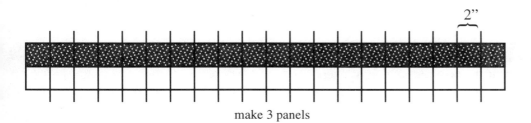

make 3 panels

cut 48

Use thirty-four each of the following to make seventeen Snail's Trail blocks: crosscut sections; dark quarter-square triangles; light quarter square triangles; dark 3 7/8" half-square triangles; and light 3 7/8" half-square triangles.

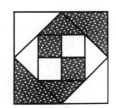

Snail's Trail
make 17

Use the remaining pieces to make fourteen Half Snail's Trail blocks, as directed below. Sew a small half-square triangle of main print fabric to each end of the remaining fourteen crosscut sections. Make sure your pieces look *exactly* like the sketch directly at the right. Press.

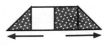

Add a quarter-square triangle of light fabric to the top of each unit from above. Press.

Now, add the large half-square triangles to the units above. Press the seam allowances toward the large triangles. Finally, sew a 3 1/2" x 6 1/2" rectangle to each pieced section, completing the Half Snail's Trail blocks. Press the seam allowances toward the rectangle.

Refer to the sketch of *On the Trail* on the previous page, and arrange the completed blocks with the remaining 6 1/2" squares of main print fabric to complete the quilt top. Some of the Snail's Trail and Half Snail's Trail blocks must be rotated a quarter or half turn to achieve the design.

Sew the blocks into horizontal rows. Press all of the seam allowances toward the Snail's Trail and Half Snail's Trail blocks. Sew the rows together. Press the seam allowances to one side.

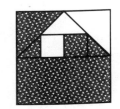

Half Snail's Trail
make 14

Homesteader's Daughters

Finished size is 49" x 61".

Fabric Requirements

Light
   2 yards

Dark fabrics - *Choose twelve pairs*
   1/4 yard of each - See cutting instructions for more information.

Backing
   3 1/8 yards

Binding
   3/4 yard

Cutting

Light
   Cut six strips 6 1/2" wide.
      Cut these strips into twenty-three 6 1/2" squares and twenty-four 3 1/2" x 6 1/2" rectangles.
   Cut fourteen 1 1/2" strips.
      Cut these strips into thirty-two rectangles of each size listed below.
         1 1/2" x 2 1/2",
         1 1/2" x 3 1/2",
         1 1/2" x 4 1/2", and
         1 1/2" x 5 1/2"
   Cut four 3 1/2" squares.

Dark fabrics

Alternating Nine Patch and Snowball blocks in this quilt gives the illusion of another traditional block, Farmer's Daughter. Each "daughter" uses two dark fabrics, a main dark (solid black in the example at the right) and a secondary dark. You may repeat the same two fabrics throughout the quilt or use twelve pairs of fabrics like the quilt on page 18.

From each of the 12 main dark fabrics
   Cut one strip 2 1/2" wide.
      Cut thirteen 2 1/2" squares from each of the twelve strips.
   Cut one strip 1 1/2" wide.

From each of the 12 secondary dark fabrics
   Cut one strip 2 1/2" wide.
      Cut six 2 1/2" squares from each of the twelve strips.
   Cut one strip 1 1/2" wide.

Cut the 1 1/2" wide strips of dark fabrics from above into thirty-two rectangles of each size listed below. If you are using many fabrics, cut some of each fabric for every size.
      1 1/2" x 3 1/2",
      1 1/2" x 4 1/2",
      1 1/2" x 5 1/2", and
      1 1/2" x 6 1/2"

Homesteader's Daughters
Layout Graphic

Piecing

Use five squares of main dark and four squares of secondary dark to piece a Nine Patch block. Repeat with the other fabrics to make a total of twelve Nine Patch blocks.

make 12

Refer to the sketch of the Homesteader's Daughters quilt and arrange the Nine Patch blocks with the squares of light fabric. Place a light fabric square in each place that there will be a Snowball block, as well as, where there is a plain block of light fabric.

Place the 3 1/2" x 6 1/2" rectangles and 3 1/2" squares of light fabric as a border around those you arranged above. Again, refer to the sketch.

Use eight 2 1/2" squares of each main dark fabric to complete the seventeen Snowball and fourteen Half Snowball blocks. See the sketch on page 31 for the correct placement of the fabrics. Refer to page 74 for Snowball piecing instructions.

Half Snowball
make 14

Piece the blocks that you've completed into horizontal rows. Press all of the seam allowances away from the Snowball or Half Snowball blocks. Sew the rows together. Press the seam allowances to one side.

Log Cabin blocks

The Log Cabin blocks are used as a pieced border for this quilt. To make your blocks faster and more precise, construct all thirty-two at the same time.

Sew a 2 1/2" square of dark fabric to each of the 1 1/2" x 2 1/2" rectangles of light fabric. Chain piece. You'll have four squares left over. Save them for future blocks.

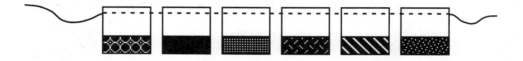

Clip the threads to separate the blocks. Press. Chain piece as you add the next piece to all thirty-two blocks. Refer to the Log Cabin block on page 53 for more instruction. Complete the blocks.

Sew the blocks into four borders like the one below. Press the seam allowances to one side.

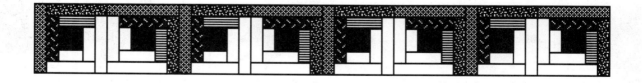

Add borders to the sides of the quilt first. Press the seam allowances away from the borders. Finally, add the top and bottom borders. Press.

Tuesday's Child

Finished size is 42" x 42".

Fabric Requirements

White
1 3/8 yards

Fat quarters and scraps of accent prints for sampler blocks
See cutting instructions.

Backing
1 3/8 yards, perhaps more if narrower than 44", or make narrower borders.

Binding
1/2 yard

Cutting

Light
Trim the selvage from one edge of the white fabric.
Cut four strips 5 1/2" wide, *lengthwise*, and reserve these for the borders.
Use the remainder of the white fabric for piecing the sampler blocks.

Prints
Each sampler block is framed with a different fabric. You'll need two 1 1/2" x 6 1/2" rectangles and two 1 1/2" x 8 1/2" rectangles of sixteen fabrics.
The remaining pieces will be cut during block construction.

Piecing

Construct sixteen blocks of your choice.

Border each block with rectangles of print fabric. Sew the 1 1/2" x 6 1/2" rectangles to opposite sides of each block. Press the seam allowances toward the rectangles. Add the 1 1/2" x 8 1/2" rectangles to the remaining two sides. Press the seam allowances toward the rectangles.

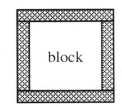
block

Set the blocks into four horizontal rows of four blocks. Sew the blocks together. Press as shown by the arrows. Sew the rows together. Press the seam allowances to one side.

HINT: If you rotate every other block a quarter turn, there will be no seams to match when you sew the blocks together. Start the odd rows with the 6 1/2" rectangle at the top of the block. Start the even rows with the 8 1/2" rectangle at the top of the block.

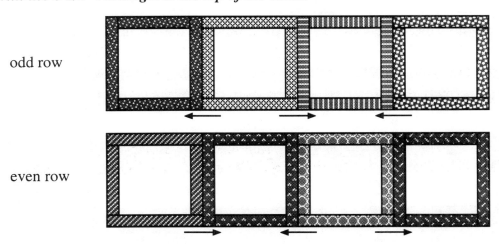

odd row

even row

Trim the reserved border strips to size and attach them to the quilt with overlapped corners.

Snips & Snails

Finished size is 40" x 40".

Fabric Requirements

Gold - *Use one or two (one for sashes and a second for blocks).*
  total of 3/4 yard - See cutting instructions.

Blue
  3/4 yard

Orange
  1/2 yard

Scraps of accent fabrics for sampler blocks

Border
  1 1/4 yards

Backing
  1 1/4 yards, perhaps more if narrower than 44"

Binding
  1/2 yard

Cutting

Gold
  Cut four strips 1 1/2" wide.

Blue
  Cut twelve strips 1 1/2" wide.

Orange
  Cut five strips 1 1/2" wide.

Border
  Trim the selvage from one edge of the border fabric.
  Cut four strips 5 1/2" wide, *lengthwise*, and reserve these for the borders.
  Use the remainder of the border fabric for piecing the sampler blocks.

Scraps of accent fabrics
  Refer to the instructions for the blocks you choose.

Piecing

Sew the 1 1/2" strips into panels like those below. The number at the left of each sketch tells you how many of each to make. Refer to the key at the right for which fabrics to use. Press.

34

Crosscut all four of Panel #1 into sections that are 6 1/2" wide. Cut twenty-four sections. These are the sashes for the quilt.

Crosscut Panels #2 and #3 into sections that are 1 1/2" wide. Cut sixteen sections from #2 and thirty-two sections from #3. Use these to construct sixteen nine patch units. These are the cornerstones for your quilt.

make 16

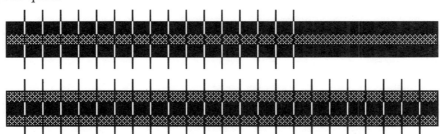

Arrange your sashes and cornerstones on a design wall. Make nine sampler blocks of your choice and put them in place on the design wall.

Assemble the quilt top by making horizontal rows. Press all of the seam allowances toward the sashes.

Sew the rows together. Press the seam allowances toward the rows that contain the nine patches.

Trim the reserved border strips, and attach them to the quilt with overlapped corners.

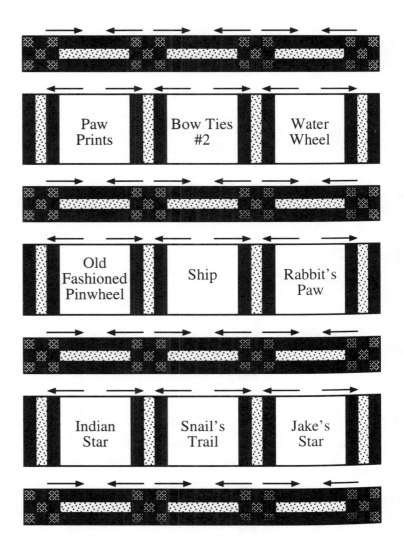

35

Who Has the Old Maid?

Finished size is 52" x 66 1/2".

Fabric Requirements

Fat quarters and scraps of fabrics for sampler block
Study Chapter 2, Fabric Selection, before beginning this quilt.

Sashing
1 yard

Border
1 5/8 yards

Backing
3 1/4 yards

Binding
3/4 yard

Cutting

Sashing
Cut fifteen strips 1 3/4" wide.
Use seven of the strips to cut forty-two 1 3/4" x 6 1/2" rectangles. The other strips will be trimmed to size when needed.

Piecing

Make seventeen pairs of blocks and an odd one (thirty-five blocks, total). My odd block was Old Maid's Puzzle. Listed below are the blocks I used. Substitute blocks you prefer, but choose ones that have a potential for making the two like blocks look very different with fabric placement. In other words, it is very difficult to make a nine patch look like anything more than a nine patch.

Dutchman's Puzzle	Double Pinwheel	Indian Star
Snail's Trail	Churn Dash	Capital T's
Paddle Wheel	Big Dipper	Country Farm
Crosses & Losses	Road to Oklahoma	Ohio Star
Milky Way	Twelve Triangles	Ribbon Star
London Roads	Evening Star	Old Maid's Puzzle

Arrange the blocks into seven horizontal rows of five blocks. Make rows, sewing a 1 3/4" x 6 1/2" strip of sashing between the blocks and at each end of the row. Press the seam allowances toward the sashes.

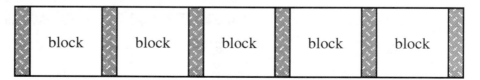

Measure the length of the rows and determine the average size. Trim the remaining eight 1 3/4" strips to this length. Sew one to the bottom of each row of blocks. Press.

This chart will help you identify the blocks in the *Who Has the Old Maid?* quilt.

Indian Star	Double Pinwheel	Capital T's	Churn Dash	Twelve Triangles
Paddle Wheel	Road to Oklahoma	Dutchman's Puzzle #1	Evening Star	Country Farm
Ribbon Star	Country Farm	Crosses & Losses	London Roads	Ohio Star
Big Dipper	Capital T's	Big Dipper	Paddle Wheel	Milky Way
Dutchman's Puzzle #1	Milky Way	Ribbon Star	Snail's Trail	Indian Star
Twelve Triangles	Old Maid's Puzzle	Double Pinwheel	Ohio Star	Churn Dash
Evening Star	London Roads	Road to Oklahoma	Snail's Trail	Crosses & Losses

Sew the rows together. This sounds easier to do than it is. When there are no cornerstones, it takes very careful pinning and sewing to keep the seam lines of the pieced rows aligned with one another.

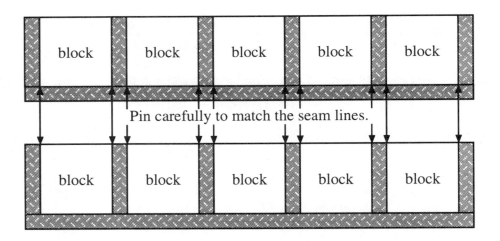

Add the last sashing strip to the top of the quilt. Press the seam allowances toward the sashing strips.

Trim the selvage from one side of the border fabric. Cut four lengthwise strips that are 7 1/2" wide. Use these to add borders with overlapped corners.

Quilting

To further enhance the difference between two blocks of the same pattern, quilt them differently. Compare the quilting lines in the two Snail's Trail blocks below. Use your imagination and let the fabrics be your guide.

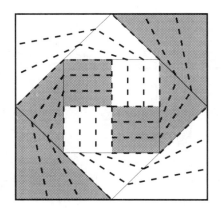
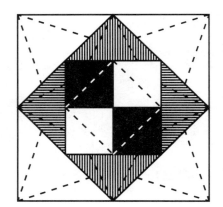

38

Sew Many Treasured Memories

Finished size is 63" x 71".

Fabric Requirements

Black for background & narrow borders
   2 1/2 yards

Fat quarters and scraps of fabrics for sampler blocks

Teal for setting triangles
   3/4 yard

Dark Purple for setting triangles
   3/4 yard

Print Border
   2 1/8 yards

Turquoise Border
   1/2 yard

Backing
   4 yards

Binding
   3/4 yard

Cutting

Black
   Cut sixteen strips 2" wide.
   Cut one strip 9 3/4" wide.
      Cut the 9 3/4" strip into three squares.
         Cut each square twice, diagonally, to make four quarter-square triangles from each.
            Yield: 12 triangles
   Cut two 5 1/8" squares.
      Cut the 5 1/8" squares once, diagonally, to make two half-square triangles from each.
         Yield: 4 triangles

Teal
   Cut four strips 5 1/8" wide.
      Cut the strips into thirty 5 1/8" squares.
         Cut each square once, diagonally, to make two half-square triangles from each.
            Yield: 60 triangles

Dark Purple
   Cut as directed for teal.

Print Border
   Trim the selvage from one edge of the border fabric.
   Cut four strips 7 1/2" wide, *lengthwise*, and reserve them for the borders.
   The remaining fabric may be used for piecing the sampler blocks.

Turquoise Border
   Cut eight strips 1 1/2" wide.

Piecing

Make twenty-three blocks of your choice. Refer to the layout sketch on page 40 for the names of those Jo Ann used. Turn each block on point and sew a half-square triangle of teal or purple to each side. Refer to the sketch at the right for the correct positions. Press the seam allowances toward the setting triangles.

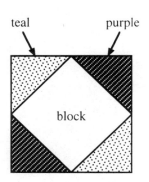

39

Use the half-square and quarter-square triangles to make the units that are shown below. Press as directed by the arrows.

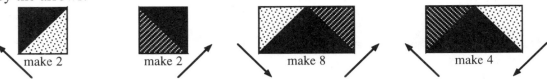

Arrange the blocks and pieced units from above. See the sketch below.

Sew the pieces into horizontal rows. Press the seam allowances to the side. Sew the rows together. Press.

Borders: Sew the sixteen 2" strips of black end to end into pairs to make them long enough for the borders. Do the same with the 1 1/2" strips of turquoise. Sew the border strips into four panels like the one below at the left. The sketches are a bit out of scale. The borders must be at least 73" long. Press the seam allowances toward the black. Attach the borders to the quilt, mitering the corners. Refer to page 10 for more instruction on mitered corner borders.

40

Ginger Snaps

Finished size is 34 1/2" x 43".

Fabric Requirements

Dark Tan
  1 1/2 yards
Light
  1 yard
Green
  3/8 yard

Fat quarters and scraps of accent fabrics for sampler blocks

Backing
  1 1/8 yards, more if it is less than 44" wide
Binding
  1/2 yard

Cutting

Dark Tan
  Cut three strips 2" wide.
  Cut three strips 3 1/2" wide.
    Cut this strip into twenty 3 1/2" squares and four 3 1/2" x 6 1/2" rectangles.
  Cut one strip 6 1/2" wide.
    Cut this strip into six 6 1/2" squares.
  Cut one strip 9 3/4" wide.
    Cut this strip into four 9 3/4" squares.
      Cut the 9 3/4" squares twice, diagonally, to make four quarter-square triangles from each.
      Yield: 16 triangles
  Cut two 5 1/8" squares.
    Cut the 5 1/8" squares once, diagonally, to make two half-square triangles from each.
    Yield: 4 triangles

Green
  Cut three strips 2" wide.

Piecing

Make twelve blocks of your choice, using the light fabric as a background in each block.

Sew the 2" strips of dark tan and green into three panels like the one below. Press.

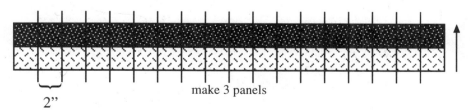

make 3 panels

Crosscut the three panels into fifty-six 2" wide sections. Use the sections to piece twenty-eight four patch units.

make 28

41

Use twenty of the four patch units and twenty 3 1/2" squares to make ten Double Four Patch blocks. See page 50 for more instruction.

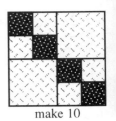
make 10

Use the remaining four patch units and the four 3 1/2" x 6 1/2" rectangles of dark tan to piece four blocks that are a variation of the Double Four Patch.

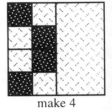
make 4

This quilt is set on point. It is pieced together by making diagonal rows. Arrange the sampler blocks, Double Four Patch blocks, and setting squares and triangles as shown below. The four half-square triangles are the corners of the quilt.

Stitch the blocks into diagonal rows. Press the seam allowances away from the sampler blocks and away from the triangles. Sew the rows together. Press the seam allowances to one side.

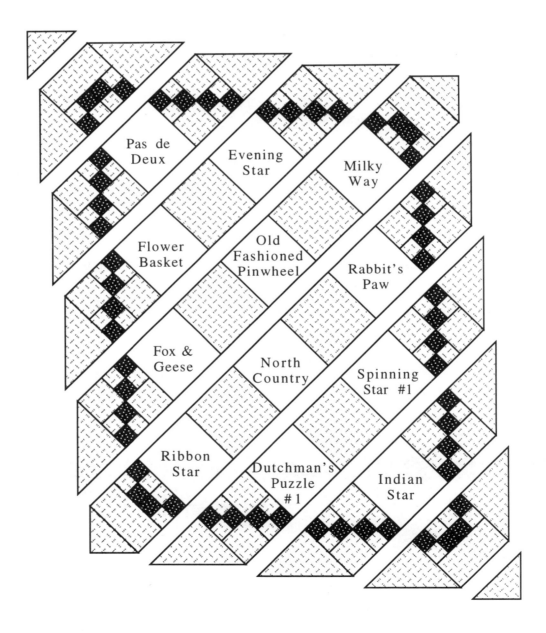

Gemstones

Finished size is 46" x 56".

Fabric Requirements

Blue-green for chains & setting triangles
  2 1/4 yards
Light
  2 1/2 yards
Fat quarters and scraps of accent fabrics for sampler blocks

Backing
  3 yards
Binding
  3/4 yard

Cutting

Blue-green
  Cut two strips 2 1/2" wide.
  Cut eight strips 1 1/2" wide.
    Cut two of the 1 1/2" strips into forty-nine 1 1/2" squares. Reserve the others for strip piecing.
  Cut two strips 15" wide.
    Cut those two strips into four 15" squares.
      Cut the 15" squares twice, diagonally, to make four quarter-square triangles from each.
        Yield: 16 triangles
  Cut two 11" squares.
    Cut the 11" squares once, diagonally, to make two half-square triangles from each.
        Yield: 4 triangles

Light
  Cut three strips 6 1/2" wide.
    Cut these strips into eighty 1 1/2" x 6 1/2" rectangles.
  Cut three strips 4 1/2" wide.
    Use one and a half of these strips to cut forty 1 1/2" x 4 1/2" rectangles. Reserve the remaining one and a half strips for strip piecing.
  Cut two strips 2 1/2" wide.
  Cut three strips 1 1/2" wide.

Piecing

Make twelve blocks of your choice, using the light fabric as the background in each.

Use three 1 1/2" strips of light and one and a half 2 1/2" strips of blue-green to piece one and a half panels like the one shown below. Press. Crosscut those panels into twenty 2 1/2" wide sections.

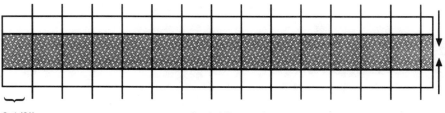

2 1/2"   make 1 1/2 panels

Use three 1 1/2" strips of blue-green and one and a half 2 1/2" strips of light to piece one and a half panels like the one shown below. Press. Crosscut those panels into forty 1 1/2" wide sections.

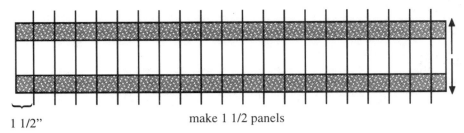

make 1 1/2 panels

Use three 1 1/2" strips of blue-green and one and a half 4 1/2" strips of light to piece one and a half panels like the one shown below. Press. Crosscut those panels into forty 1 1/2" wide sections.

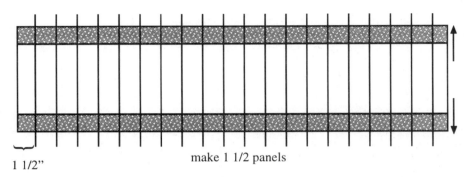

make 1 1/2 panels

Arrange the crosscut sections from the last three steps with the forty 1 1/2" x 4 1/2" rectangles of light to make twenty Linking Squares blocks. For more details see page 52.

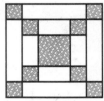

make 20

Arrange the twelve sampler blocks, twenty Linking Squares blocks, the sashings, cornerstones, and setting triangles to complete the quilt top. The sashing and cornerstones make this setting a little more challenging than the on point setting of the *Ginger Snaps* quilt, but take it one step at a time and you will breeze through it!

Set aside the four corner triangles. These will be added last. Now, focus on Row 1. See the sketch on the next page. Sew a cornerstone to each end of a sash. Sew a sash to each side of a Linking Squares block. During the construction of the rows, press all seam allowances toward the sashes. Sew these two sections together. Press the seam allowances toward the sashing row. Add a quarter-square triangle to each side of this pieced section, aligning the square corners at the bottom and allowing the points to extend beyond the top, as shown in the third sketch. Press. Trim, as indicated by the dotted line. Row 9 is constructed exactly like Row 1.

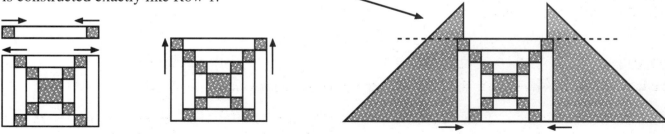

Rows 2 and 8 are completed as shown below. Add triangles and trim as before.

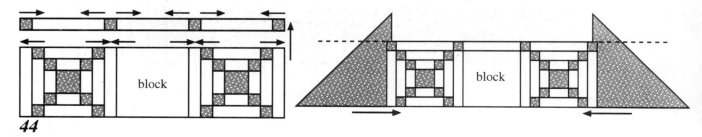

44

Rows 3 and 7 are exactly the same. Make them as you have the previous ones. Refer to the sketch at the bottom of this page for block and sashing placement.

Rows 4 and 6 are alike, and have triangles on only one end. Refer to the sketch below to piece these rows. Press.

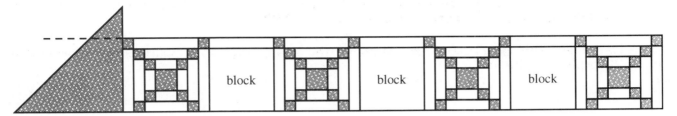

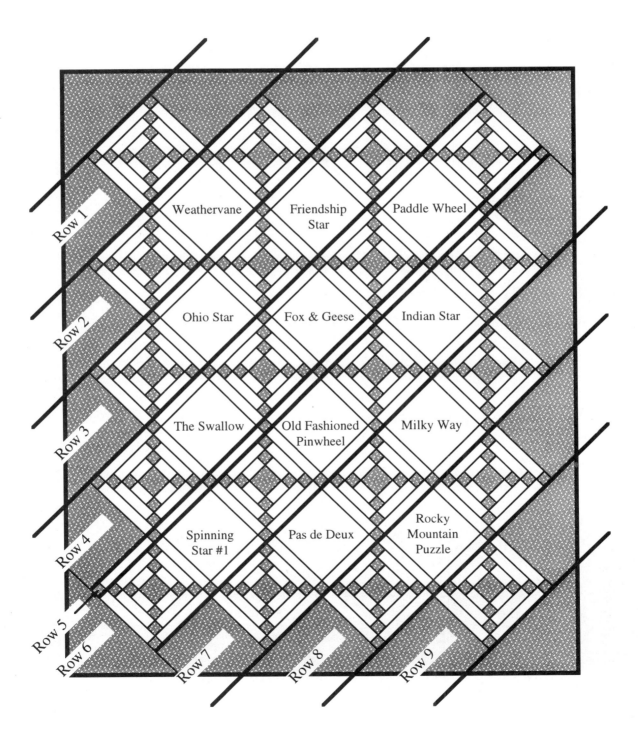

Make Row 5. Press.

Sew Rows 1 through 4 together. Sew Rows 6 through 9 together. Press all of the seam allowances away from the center of the quilt. Attach the two halves of the quilt to Row 5. Press.

Finally, trim the setting triangles, as needed, to add the four half-square triangles to the corners of the quilt. Press the seam allowances toward the corners.

If necessary, trim the outside edges to even them. The setting triangles are purposely oversized to omit the addition of a border.

Q-Bert

Finished size is 38" x 38".

Fabric Requirements

Dark Background
 1 1/4 yards

Light
 1 yard

Accent fabrics for blocks
 Fat quarters or scraps, see cutting instructions

Medium Teal for setting
 1/4 yard

Medium-Dark Teal for setting
 1/4 yard

Backing
 1 1/4 yards

Binding
 1/2 yard

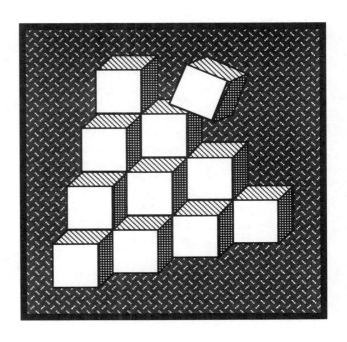

Cutting

Medium Teal
 Cut two strips 2 1/2" wide.

Medium-Dark Teal
 Cut two strips 2 1/2" wide.

Piecing

Make ten or eleven blocks of your choice. Placing an extra block in a tumbling position can add interest to your quilt. See the graphic above.

Open the four strips of sashing *completely*. Leaving them folded will create reverse pieces that will not work. Pair one strip of each fabric (medium teal and medium-dark teal), RST. **With the lighter fabric on top, cut a 45 degree angle through the pair on one end, as shown.** Reversing the fabrics or direction of the 45 degree angle will change the placement of the sashing. It may change the "light source" or stacking arrangement, as well. Follow these instructions carefully, or you may be designing on your own.

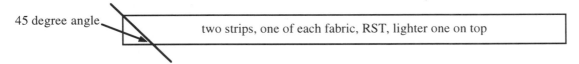

Use your rotary cutter and ruler to cut ten or eleven sections, one for each block, that are 4 3/4" wide. See the sketch below. Use both strips of each color.

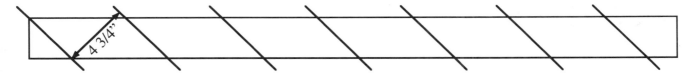

47

Sew the parallelograms into pairs. Start your stitching on the 1/4" seam line, as indicated by the arrow. Make a few stitches, backstitch, and sew to the end of the seam line. Press the seam allowances open.

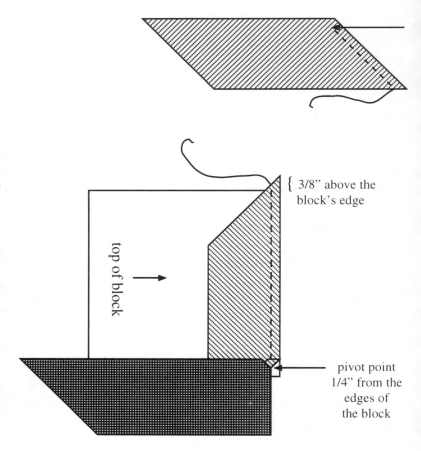

Set a block into each sashing pair, making sure the block is rotated correctly so that it will be right side up once the sashing is sewn on. This is a set-in seam. Read through the rest of these instructions before continuing.

Place the block right side up. Put the sashing, RST, on the block, aligning the edge of the medium teal parallelogram with the top of the block. See the sketch at the right. Notice how far the teal piece extends beyond the block at the beginning of the stitching line, and how it aligns at the pivot point.

Begin stitching and stop with the needle down in the fabrics after sewing for about an inch. Fold the medium-dark teal parallelogram to the left, as shown in the second sketch. This is like opening the front cover of a book. Check the alignment at the pivot point and pin, if necessary. Stitch to the pivot point, where your needle is just beyond the medium teal piece and in the block fabric, only. Stop with the needle down.

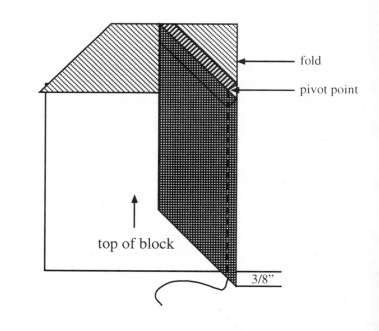

Lift the presser foot, reach under, and pull the second side of the block toward you, in a counter-clockwise direction, a quarter turn. This will put the second side in position to be sewn. Push the medium teal parallelogram backward in a clockwise direction until the raw edge of the medium-dark teal piece will align with the edge of the block. ***Make sure that the second parallelogram is close enough to the needle so that the first stitch you take will catch it.***

Lower the presser foot and ***take one stitch***. If you have stitched through the parallelogram, align the remainder of the two edges, easing, if necessary, and finish the seam. Taking several stitches before stitching into the parallelogram will cause a hole or gap in the corner.

Press the seam allowances away from the block. Trim the dog ears. Sew sashing to all of the blocks in the same way.

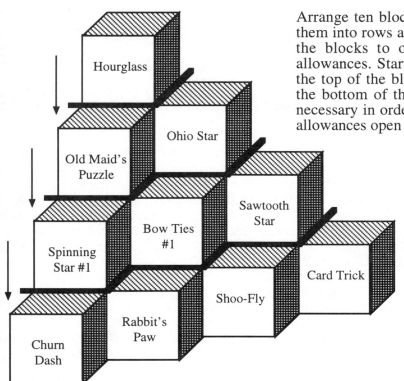

Arrange ten blocks in a stack like the one at the left. Sew them into rows as defined by the heavy lines. As you stitch the blocks to one another, do not stitch in the seam allowances. Start on the seam line, 1/4" from the edge, at the top of the block, and end on the seam line, 1/4" from the bottom of the block. Backstitch at both ends. This is necessary in order to sew the rows together. Press all seam allowances open after sewing the blocks into rows.

Sew the rows together. This is not an easy task. Pin at the corners, and stitch carefully. It may be easier to pin and stitch one short section; stop, pin, and stitch the next one; etc. For instance, sew the bottom two rows together with six short seams. Press the seam allowances all toward the bottom row.

Staystitch a scant 1/4" around the outside of the stack of blocks. Press the seam allowance under.

Center the stack of blocks on a 40" square of dark background fabric. Keep the sides of the blocks parallel to the sides of the background. Pin.

Applique the block section in place by hand or machine. From the back trim out the dark background from behind the stack of blocks.

Staystitch the edges of an eleventh block, and applique it precariously on the stack for a touch of whimsy.

49

Chapter 4
Block Construction

Each block is shown in a line drawing and in a second sketch showing a traditional placement of fabrics. Use the value placements only as suggestions. Refer to the photos of the quilts for more ideas. Be creative with your fabric choices. At the end of this chapter you will find four pages of line drawings that can be photocopied for your personal use. These are very helpful when trying to imagine other fabric arrangements while making the puzzle quilt, *Who Has the Old Maid?*.

The small arrows in the sketches are suggested pressing directions. I choose to press my pieces in the direction that is best for eliminating bulk and making the seams butt together for ease in matching. This is not always toward the darker fabric.

Please take the time to read Chapter 1 prior to piecing your blocks. It contains valuable information about cutting, pressing, and piecing techniques.

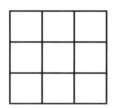 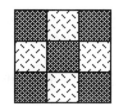

Nine Patch

Light
  Cut four 2 1/2" squares.

Dark
  Cut five 2 1/2" squares.

Arrange the squares into three rows of three squares. Sew them together into three horizontal rows. Press the seam allowances of the top and bottom rows away from the center square. Press the seam allowances of the middle row toward the center square. Sew the rows together, matching the seam lines. Press the seam allowances away from the middle row.

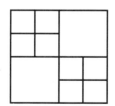 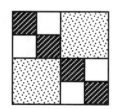

Double Four Patch

Light
  Cut four 2" squares.

Medium
  Cut two 3 1/2" squares.

Dark
  Cut four 2" squares.

Use the 2" squares of light and dark to make two four patch units. Press as shown by the arrows. Arrange the four patch units and the 3 1/2" squares to make a Double Four Patch block. Sew two horizontal rows. Press the seam allowances toward the 3 1/2" square of medium fabric in each row. Sew the two rows together. Press the seam allowances to one side.

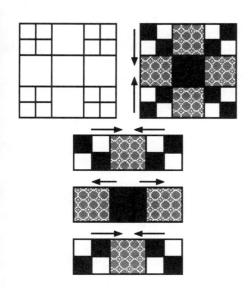

Marching Band

Light
　Cut eight 1 1/2" squares.

Medium
　Cut four 2 1/2" squares.

Dark
　Cut eight 1 1/2" squares.
　Cut one 2 1/2" square.

Use the sixteen 1 1/2" squares to make four four patch units. Refer to the Double Four Patch block for more instruction.

Arrange the four patch units with the remaining squares. Complete the block, as directed for the Nine Patch block, but press the seam allowances in the directions shown by the arrows.

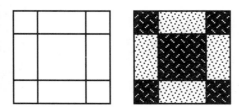

Puss in the Corner #1

Light
　Cut four 2" x 3 1/2" rectangles.

Dark
　Cut four 2" squares.
　Cut one 3 1/2" square.

Arrange the squares and rectangles. Complete the block as directed for the Nine Patch block.

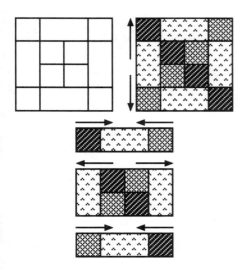

Ups & Downs

Light
　Cut four 2" x 3 1/2" rectangles.

Medium
　Cut four 2" squares.

Dark
　Cut four 2" squares.

Use two 2" squares of medium and two 2" squares of dark to piece a four patch unit for the center of the block. Refer to the Double Four Patch block for more instruction.

Arrange the four patch unit and remaining pieces to make the Ups & Downs block. Complete the block as directed for the Nine Patch block, but refer to the arrows for pressing directions.

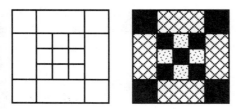

Cornered Nine Patch

Light
　Cut four 1 1/2" squares.

Medium
　Cut four 2" x 3 1/2" rectangles.

Dark
　Cut four 2" squares.
　Cut five 1 1/2" squares.

Use the nine 1 1/2" squares to make a nine patch unit. Refer to the Nine Patch block for more instruction. Complete and press the block as directed for the Ups & Downs block, using the nine patch unit to replace the four patch unit in the center.

Chain

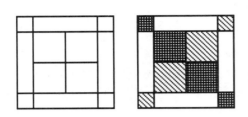

Light
    Cut four 1 1/2" x 4 1/2" rectangles.
Medium
    Cut two 2 1/2" squares.
    Cut two 1 1/2" squares.
Dark
    Cut two 2 1/2" squares.
    Cut two 1 1/2" squares.

Arrange the squares and rectangles. Piece and press the block as directed for the Ups & Downs block.

Linking Squares

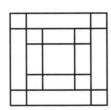 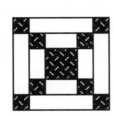

Light
    Cut four 1 1/2" x 2 1/2" rectangles.
    Cut four 1 1/2" x 4 1/2" rectangles.
Dark
    Cut eight 1 1/2" squares.
    Cut one 2 1/2" square.

Use four 1 1/2" squares of dark, the 2 1/2" square of dark, and four 1 1/2" x 2 1/2" rectangles of light to piece the Puss in a Corner unit in the center of the block. Refer to the Puss in the Corner #1 block for more instruction. Arrange the center unit and remaining pieces to complete the block. Piece and press the block as directed for the Ups & Downs block.

Up the Down Staircase

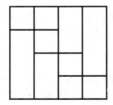 

Lights
    Cut one 2" square.
    Cut one 2" x 3 1/2" rectangle.
    Cut one 2" x 5" rectangle.
Darks
    Same as lights.
Contrast
    Cut four 2" squares.

Arrange the pieces as shown. Sew them into four vertical rows. Press all seam allowances toward the contrasting fabric. Sew the rows together. Press the seam allowances to one side.

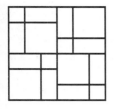
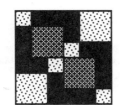

Patience Corners

Light
>Cut two 2 1/2" squares.
>Cut four 1 1/2" squares.

Medium
>Cut two 2 1/2" squares.

Dark
>Cut eight 1 1/2" x 2 1/2" rectangles.

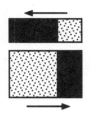

Use one 1 1/2" square, two rectangles, and one 2 1/2" square to make a unit like the one at the left. Repeat with the remaining pieces to make three more units. Two of the four units will use a 2 1/2" square of medium fabric. Arrange the four units to make a Patience Corners block. Complete the block as directed for the Pinwheel #1 block below.

Log Cabin

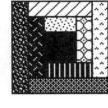

Lights
>Cut one 1 1/2" x 2 1/2" rectangle (#1).
>Cut one 1 1/2" x 3 1/2" rectangle (#2).
>Cut one 1 1/2" x 4 1/2" rectangle (#5).
>Cut one 1 1/2" x 5 1/2" rectangle (#6).

Darks
>Cut one 1 1/2" x 3 1/2" rectangle (#3).
>Cut one 1 1/2" x 4 1/2" rectangle (#4).
>Cut one 1 1/2" x 5 1/2" rectangle (#7).
>Cut one 1 1/2" x 6 1/2" rectangle (#8).

Contrast
>Cut one 2 1/2" square (C).

Add the rectangles to the 2 1/2" square of contrasting fabric in the order they are numbered. Press the seam allowances away from the center square after each piece is added.

Pinwheel #1

Light
>Cut two 3 7/8" squares.
>>Cut the squares once, diagonally, to make two half-square triangles from each.
>>>Yield: 4 triangles

Dark
>Same as light.

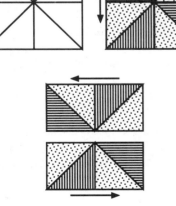

Sew a dark triangle to each light triangle along the long bias edge. Press the seam allowances toward the dark fabric. Arrange the four units to make a Pinwheel #1 block, and sew them together as you would a four patch block. Make two horizontal rows. Press the seam allowances of the top and bottom rows in opposite directions. Press the last seam allowance to one side.

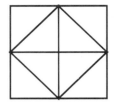 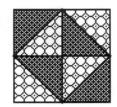

Broken Dishes

Light
  Cut two 3 7/8" squares.
    Cut the squares once, diagonally, to make two half-square triangles from each.
      Yield: 4 triangles

Dark
  Same as light.

Sew a dark triangle to each light triangle along the long bias edge. Press the seam allowances toward the dark fabric. Arrange the four units to make a Broken Dishes block. Complete the block as directed for the Pinwheel #1 block.

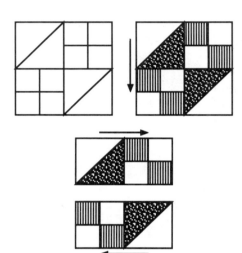

Anvil

Light
  Cut four 2" squares.
  Cut one 3 7/8" square.
    Cut the 3 7/8" square once, diagonally, to make two half-square triangles.
      Yield: 2 triangles

Medium
  Cut four 2" squares.

Dark
  Cut one 3 7/8" square.
    Cut the square once, diagonally, to make two half-square triangles.
      Yield: 2 triangles

Use the squares to make two four patch units. Refer to the Double Four Patch block for more instruction. Use the triangles to make two half-square triangle units. Press the seam allowances toward the dark fabric. Arrange the four units to make an Anvil block. Complete the block, pressing the pieces as shown by the arrows.

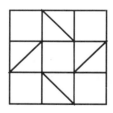 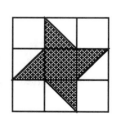

Friendship Star

Light
  Cut four 2 1/2" squares.
  Cut two 2 7/8" squares.
    Cut the 2 7/8" squares once, diagonally, to make two half-square triangles from each.
      Yield: 4 triangles

Dark
  Cut one 2 1/2" square.
  Cut two 2 7/8" squares.
    Cut the 2 7/8" squares once, diagonally, to make two half-square triangles from each.
      Yield: 4 triangles

Use the triangles to make four half-square triangle units. Press. Arrange the half-square triangle units and the remaining squares to make a Friendship Star block. Complete the block as directed for the Nine Patch block.

Shoo-Fly

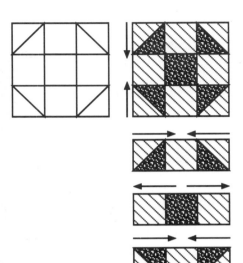

Light
- Cut four 2 1/2" squares.
- Cut two 2 7/8" squares.
  - Cut the 2 7/8" squares once, diagonally, to make two half-square triangles from each.
    - Yield: 4 triangles

Dark
- Cut one 2 1/2" square.
- Cut two 2 7/8" squares.
  - Cut the 2 7/8" squares once, diagonally, to make two half-square triangles from each.
    - Yield: 4 triangles

Use the triangles to make four half-square triangle units. Press. Arrange the half-square triangle units and the remaining squares to make a Shoo-Fly block. Complete the block as directed for the Nine Patch block, but refer to the arrows for pressing directions.

Split Nine Patch

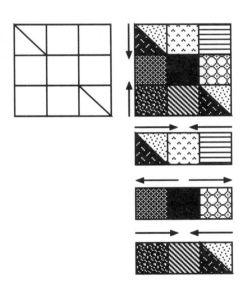

Lights
- Cut three 2 1/2" squares.
- Cut one 2 7/8" square.
  - Cut the 2 7/8" square once, diagonally, to make two half-square triangles.
    - Yield: 2 triangles

Darks
- Cut four 2 1/2" squares.
- Cut one 2 7/8" square.
  - Cut the 2 7/8" square once, diagonally, to make two half-square triangles.
    - Yield: 2 triangles

Use the triangles to make two half-square triangle units. Press. Arrange the half-square triangle units and the remaining squares to make a Split Nine Patch block. Complete the block as directed for the Nine Patch block, but refer to the arrows for pressing directions.

Contrary Wife

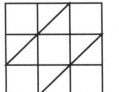 

Light
- Cut two 2 1/2" squares.
- Cut two 2 7/8" squares.
  - Cut the 2 7/8" squares once, diagonally, to make two half-square triangles from each.
    - Yield: 4 triangles

55

Medium
Cut two 2 7/8" squares.
Cut the squares once, diagonally, to make two half-square triangles from each.
Yield: 4 triangles

Dark
Cut three 2 1/2" squares.

Use the triangles to make four half-square triangle units. Press. Arrange the half-square triangle units and the remaining squares to make a Contrary Wife block. Complete the block as directed for the Nine Patch block.

Three & Six

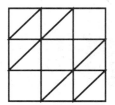
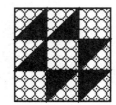

Light
Cut three 2 1/2" squares.
Cut three 2 7/8" squares.
Cut the 2 7/8" squares once, diagonally, to make two half-square triangles from each.
Yield: 6 triangles

Darks
Cut three 2 7/8" squares.
Cut the squares once, diagonally, to make two half-square triangles from each.
Yield: 6 triangles

Use the triangles to make six half-square triangle units. Press. Arrange the half-square triangle units and the remaining squares to make a Three & Six block. Complete the block as directed for the Nine Patch block.

Churn Dash

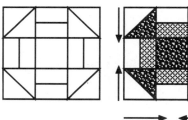

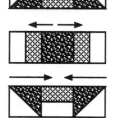

Light
Cut four 1 1/2" x 2 1/2" rectangles.
Cut two 2 7/8" squares.
Cut the squares once, diagonally, to make two half-square triangles from each.
Yield: 4 triangles

Medium
Cut four 1 1/2" x 2 1/2" rectangles.

Dark
Cut one 2 1/2" square.
Cut two 2 7/8" squares.
Cut the 2 7/8" squares once, diagonally, to make two half-square triangles from each.
Yield: 4 triangles

Use the triangles to make four half-square triangle units. Press. Sew a light rectangle to each medium rectangle along one long edge. Press. Arrange the half-square triangle units, the units made with the rectangles, and the remaining square to make a Churn Dash block. Complete the block as directed for the Nine Patch block, but refer to the arrows for pressing directions.

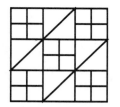 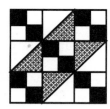

Jacob's Ladder

Light
    Cut ten 1 1/2" squares.
    Cut two 2 7/8" squares.
        Cut the 2 7/8" squares once, diagonally, to make two half-square triangles from each.
                Yield: 4 triangles

Medium
    Cut two 2 7/8" squares.
        Cut the squares once, diagonally, to make two half-square triangles from each.
                Yield: 4 triangles

Dark
    Cut ten 1 1/2" squares.

Use the triangles to make four half-square triangle units. Press. Make five four patch units from the 1 1/2" squares of dark and light. Refer to the Double Four Patch block for more instruction. Arrange the four patches and the half-square triangle units to make a Jacob's Ladder block. Complete the block as directed for the Nine Patch block.

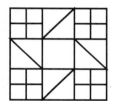 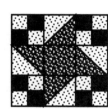

Water Wheel

Light
    Cut eight 1 1/2" squares.
    Cut two 2 7/8" squares.
        Cut the 2 7/8" squares once, diagonally, to make two half-square triangles from each.
                Yield: 4 triangles

Medium
    Cut one 2 1/2" square.
    Cut two 2 7/8" squares.
        Cut the 2 7/8" squares once, diagonally, to make two half-square triangles from each.
                Yield: 4 triangles

Dark
    Cut eight 1 1/2" squares.

Use the triangles to make four half-square triangle units. Press. Make four four patch units from the 1 1/2" squares of dark and light. Refer to the Double Four Patch block for more instruction. Arrange the pieced units and 2 1/2" square to make a Water Wheel block. Complete the block as directed for the Nine Patch block.

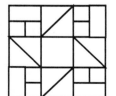 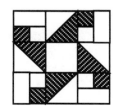

Milky Way

Light
    Cut four 1 1/2" squares.
    Cut four 1 1/2" x 2 1/2" rectangles.
    Cut one 2 1/2" square.
    Cut two 2 7/8" squares.
        Cut the 2 7/8" squares once, diagonally, to make two half-square triangles from each.
                Yield: 4 triangles

Dark
　　Cut four 1 1/2" squares.
　　Cut two 2 7/8" squares.
　　　　Cut the 2 7/8" squares once, diagonally, to make
　　　　two half-square triangles from each.
　　　　　　　　　　　　　　　　Yield: 4 triangles

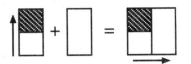

Use the triangles to make four half-square triangle units. Press. Use the small squares and rectangles to make four units like those shown directly to the left. Arrange all of the pieced units and the remaining square to make a Milky Way block. Complete the block as directed for the Nine Patch block.

Ribbon Star

 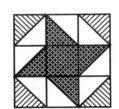

Light
　　Cut four 2 7/8" squares.
　　　　Cut the squares once, diagonally, to make two
　　　　half-square triangles from each.
　　　　　　　　　　　　　　　　Yield: 8 triangles

Medium
　　Cut two 2 7/8" squares.
　　　　Cut the squares once, diagonally, to make two
　　　　half-square triangles from each.
　　　　　　　　　　　　　　　　Yield: 4 triangles

Dark
　　Cut one 2 1/2" square.
　　Cut two 2 7/8" squares.
　　　　Cut the 2 7/8" squares once, diagonally, to make
　　　　two half-square triangles from each.
　　　　　　　　　　　　　　　　Yield: 4 triangles

Use the triangles to make four half-square triangle units of each combination shown. Press. Arrange the remaining square and the half-square triangle units to make a Ribbon Star block. Complete the block as directed for the Nine Patch block.

Puss in the Corner #2

Light
　　Cut four 2" x 3 1/2" rectangles.
　　Cut two 2 3/8" squares.
　　　　Cut the squares once, diagonally, to make two
　　　　half-square triangles from each.
　　　　　　　　　　　　　　　　Yield: 4 triangles

Dark
　　Cut one 3 1/2" square.
　　Cut two 2 3/8" squares.
　　　　Cut the 2 3/8" squares once, diagonally, to make
　　　　two half-square triangles from each.
　　　　　　　　　　　　　　　　Yield: 4 triangles

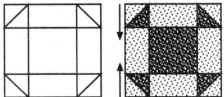
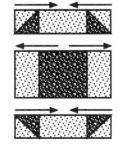

Use the triangles to make four half-square triangle units. Press. Arrange these units and the remaining pieces to make a Puss in the Corner #2 block. Complete the block as directed for the Nine Patch block, but refer to the arrows for pressing directions.

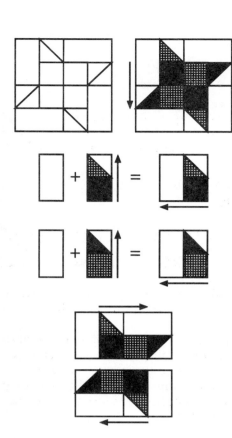

Laced Star

Light
    Cut four 2" x 3 1/2" rectangles.
    Cut two 2 3/8" squares.
        Cut the squares once, diagonally, to make two half-square triangles from each.
                      Yield: 4 triangles

Medium
    Cut two 2" squares.
    Cut one 2 3/8" square.
        Cut the 2 3/8" square once, diagonally, to make two half-square triangles.
                      Yield: 2 triangles

Dark
    Cut two 2" squares.
    Cut one 2 3/8" square.
        Cut the 2 3/8" square once, diagonally, to make two half-square triangles.
                      Yield: 2 triangles

Use the triangles to make four half-square triangle units, pairing the light triangles with either a medium or dark triangle. Press. Arrange the remaining squares, rectangles, and the half-square triangle units to make a Laced Star block. Piece the block by making the four quarters, two of each combination. Press. Complete the block as shown. Press.

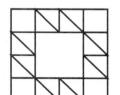

The Swallow

Light
    Cut two 2" squares.
    Cut four 2 3/8" squares.
        Cut the 2 3/8" squares once, diagonally, to make two half-square triangles from each.
                      Yield: 8 triangles

Medium
    Cut one 3 1/2" square.

Dark
    Cut two 2" squares.
    Cut four 2 3/8" squares.
        Cut the 2 3/8" squares once, diagonally, to make two half-square triangles from each.
                      Yield: 8 triangles

Use the triangles to make eight half-square triangle units. Press. Sew the half-square units into pairs, making two of each, as shown directly to the left.

Make two of each section. After sewing the half-square units into pairs, press the seam allowances open.

HINT: I prefer to press the last seam allowance, and any in other similar "sawtooth-like" sections, open. If you have not read the pressing and cutting information in Chapter 1, I suggest you take the time.

Arrange the pieced units and remaining squares to make The Swallow block. Complete the block as directed for the Nine Patch block.

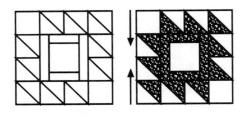

Rocky Mountain Puzzle

Light
    Cut one 2 1/2" square.
    Cut two 2" squares.
    Cut five 2 3/8" squares.
        Cut the 2 3/8" squares once, diagonally, to make two half-square triangles from each.
                      Yield: 10 triangles

Dark
    Cut two 1" x 2 1/2" rectangles.
    Cut two 1" x 3 1/2" rectangles.
    Cut five 2 3/8" squares.
        Cut the squares once, diagonally, to make two half-square triangles from each.
                      Yield: 10 triangles

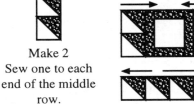

Make 2
Sew one to each end of the middle row.

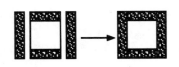

Use the triangles to make ten half-square triangle units. Press the seam allowances toward the dark or open to eliminate bulk.

Sew the two smaller rectangles of dark fabric to opposite sides of the 2 1/2" square. Press. Sew the remaining two rectangles to the other two sides of that square to complete the center of the block. Press. Sew two pairs of half-square triangle units, press the seam allowances open, and attach them to opposite sides of the center section to complete the middle row. Press.

Arrange the remaining squares and the half-square triangle units to make the top and bottom rows. Press as shown by the arrows, or open. Sew the rows together to complete the block. Press.

Crosses & Losses

Light
    Cut four 2" squares.
    Cut two 2 3/8" squares.
        Cut the 2 3/8" squares once, diagonally, to make two half-square triangles from each.
                      Yield: 4 triangles
    Cut one 3 7/8" square.
        Cut the 3 7/8" square once, diagonally, to make two half-square triangles.
                      Yield: 2 triangles

Medium
    Cut one 3 7/8" square.
        Cut the square once, diagonally, to make two half-square triangles.
                      Yield: 2 triangles

Dark
    Cut two 2 3/8" squares.
        Cut the squares once, diagonally, to make two half-square triangles from each.
                      Yield: 4 triangles

Use the triangles to make four small half-square triangle units and two large half-square triangle units. Press.

60

Make two four patch units with the small half-square triangle units and the remaining squares of light fabric. Arrange the sections to make a Crosses & Losses block. Complete the block as directed for the Pinwheel #1 block.

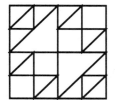
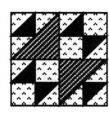

Fox & Geese

Light
   Cut four 2" squares.
   Cut five 2 3/8" squares.
      Cut the 2 3/8" squares once, diagonally, to make two half-square triangles from each.
                              Yield: 10 triangles

Medium
   Cut one 3 7/8" square.
      Cut the square once, diagonally, to make two half-square triangles.
                              Yield: 2 triangles

Dark
   Cut three 2 3/8" squares.
      Cut the squares once, diagonally, to make two half-square triangles from each.
                              Yield: 6 triangles

Use six light and six dark 2 3/8" triangles to make six small half-square triangle units. Press. Sew a small triangle of light fabric onto two of the half-square triangles to make two sections like the one directly at the left. Press the seam allowances toward the triangle you just added.

HINT: *For precision in piecing these sections, make sure you have read Chapter 1.*

Add another small triangle of light to the adjacent side of each of the two units from above. See left. Press the seam allowances toward the triangle you just added. Add a large triangle to each of these pieced units. Use the remaining four half-square triangle units and squares to make two four patch units. Refer to the Crosses & Losses block for more instruction. Arrange all of the sections to make a Fox & Geese block. Complete the block as directed for the Crosses & Losses block.

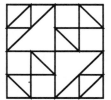
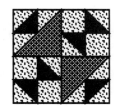

Old Maid's Puzzle

Cutting
   Follow the instructions for the Fox & Geese block above.

Piece this block exactly like the Fox & Geese block, except rotate the four patch units a quarter turn to make the block look like those at the left.

61

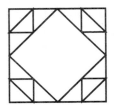 

Flower Pot

Light
> Cut six 2 3/8" squares.
>> Cut the squares once, diagonally, to make two half-square triangles from each.
>>> Yield: 12 triangles

Medium
> Cut one 4 3/4" square.

Dark
> Cut two 2 3/8" squares.
>> Cut the squares once, diagonally, to make two half-square triangles from each.
>>> Yield: 4 triangles

 Make four sections like the one at the left. Refer to the Fox & Geese block for more instruction. Sew one of these units to each side of the square. Refer to *Chapter 1*, for more information about piecing. Press the seam allowances away from the center square.

Birds in the Air #1

Light
> Cut six 2 3/8" squares.
>> Cut the squares once, diagonally, to make two half-square triangles from each.
>>> Yield: 12 triangles

Medium
> Cut two 3 7/8" squares.
>> Cut the squares once, diagonally, to make two half-square triangles from each.
>>> Yield: 4 triangles

Dark
> Cut two 2 3/8" squares.
>> Cut the squares once, diagonally, to make two half-square triangles from each.
>>> Yield: 4 triangles

 Make four units like the one at the left. Refer to the Fox & Geese block for more instruction. The unit at the left is called Bird in the Air. Arrange the four units to make the Birds in the Air #1 block. Complete the block as directed for the Double Four Patch block.

Birds in the Air #2

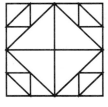 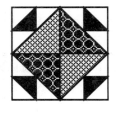

Cutting
> Follow the instructions for the Birds in the Air #1 block above, except use two different medium fabrics, cutting one 3 7/8" square from each.

Piece this block exactly like the Birds in the Air #1 block, but rotate the "birds" to make the block look like those at the left.

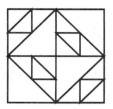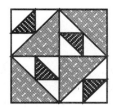

Birds in the Air #3

Cutting
Follow the instructions for the Birds in the Air #1 block on the previous page.

Piece this block exactly like the Birds in the Air #1 block, except rotate the "birds" to make the block look like those at the left.

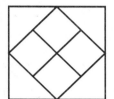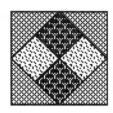

Four on Point

Light
Cut two 2 5/8" squares.

Medium
Cut two 3 7/8" squares.
Cut the squares once, diagonally, to make two half-square triangles from each.
Yield: 4 triangles

Dark
Cut two 2 5/8" squares.

Use the four squares to make a four patch unit. Press. Add a triangle of medium fabric to each side of the four patch, pressing the seam allowances toward each triangle after it is added.

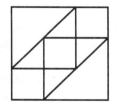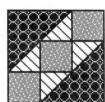

Country Pathway

Light
Cut two 2 7/8" squares.
Cut the squares once, diagonally, to make two half-square triangles from each.
Yield: 4 triangles

Medium
Cut three 2 1/2" squares.

Dark
Cut one 4 7/8" square.
Cut the square once, diagonally, to make two half-square triangles.
Yield: 2 triangles

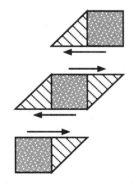

Piece the diagonal center row of this block as shown at the left. Press the seam allowances as shown by the arrows.

Press carefully to avoid stretching the bias edges of the triangles. If you have not read Chapter 1, I urge you to take the time to do so. It contains detailed information about how to sew triangles to squares precisely.

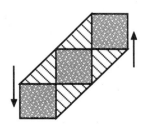

Add the large triangles to each side of the diagonal center row. Press the seam allowances toward the large triangles.

63

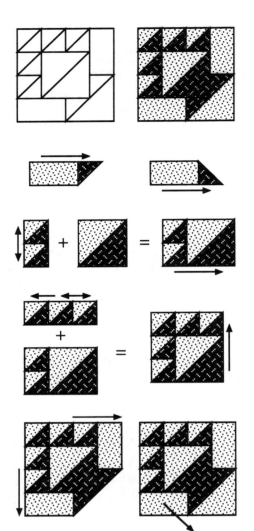

Flower Basket

Light
    Cut two 2" x 3 1/2" rectangles.
    Cut three 2 3/8" squares.
        Cut the 2 3/8" squares once, diagonally, to make two half-square triangles from each.
                Yield: 6 triangles
    Cut one 3 7/8" square.
        Cut the 3 7/8" square once, diagonally, to make two half-square triangles.
                Yield: 2 triangles

Dark
    Cut four 2 3/8" squares.
        Cut the 2 3/8" squares once, diagonally, to make two half-square triangles from each.
                Yield: 8 triangles

    Cut one 3 7/8" square.
        Cut the 3 7/8" square once, diagonally, to make two half-square triangles.
                Yield: 2 triangles

Use five small triangles of dark fabric and five small triangles of light to piece five half-square triangle units. Press. Use one large triangle of light and one large triangle of dark to piece one large half-square triangle unit. Press. Use the two rectangles and two of the small dark triangles to piece the two sections like those just below the block sketches at the upper left.

Finish piecing the block following the sketches at the left. Press after each step. I press those places that have an arrow with heads on both ends open. There will be one small light triangle, one small dark triangle, and one large dark triangle left over. Label them with their sizes and keep them handy for future blocks.

Cake Stand

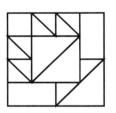 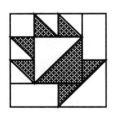

Light
    Cut two 2" x 3 1/2" rectangles.
    Cut one 2" square.
    Cut two 2 3/8" squares.
        Cut the 2 3/8" squares once, diagonally, to make two half-square triangles from each.
                Yield: 4 triangles
    Cut one 3 7/8" square.
        Cut the 3 7/8" square once, diagonally, to make two half-square triangles.
                Yield: 2 triangles

Dark
    Cut three 2 3/8" squares.
        Cut the 2 3/8" squares once, diagonally, to make two half-square triangles from each.
                Yield: 6 triangles
    Cut one 3 7/8" square.
        Cut the 3 7/8" square once, diagonally, to make two half-square triangles.
                Yield: 2 triangles

The Cake Stand block is pieced just like the Flower Basket, except you only need four small half-square triangle units. A 2" square replaces the fifth one. Rotate the small half-square triangles to create the Cake Stand block. Refer to the Flower Basket block for more instruction.

Big Dipper

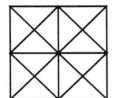 

Lights
Cut two 4 1/4" squares.
Cut the squares twice, diagonally, to make four quarter-square triangles from each.
Yield: 8 triangles

Darks
Cut two 4 1/4" squares.
Cut the squares twice, diagonally, to make four quarter-square triangles from each.
Yield: 8 triangles

 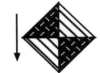

Sew the light and dark triangles into pairs. Press. Sew the pairs together to make four quarters of the block. Press. Arrange the quarters to make the Big Dipper block. Complete the block as directed for the Pinwheel #1 block.

Double Pinwheel

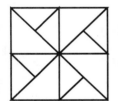 

Light
Cut one 4 1/4" square.
Cut the square twice, diagonally, to make four quarter-square triangles.
Yield: 4 triangles

Medium
Cut two 3 7/8" squares.
Cut the squares once, diagonally, to make two half-square triangles from each.
Yield: 4 triangles

Dark
Cut one 4 1/4" square.
Cut the square twice, diagonally, to make four quarter-square triangles.
Yield: 4 triangles

 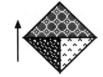

Sew the quarter-square triangles into pairs. Press. Add a half-square triangle to each pair of quarter-square triangles. Press. Arrange the units to make the Double Pinwheel block. Complete the block as directed for the Pinwheel #1 block.

Pinwheel on Point

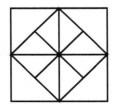 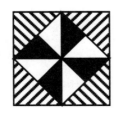

Cutting
Follow the instructions for the Double Pinwheel block above.

Piece this block exactly like the Double Pinwheel block, except rotate the four pieced units to make a block like those at the left.

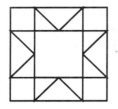 

Sawtooth Star

Light
- Cut four 2" squares.
- Cut one 4 1/4" square.
  - Cut the 4 1/4" square twice, diagonally, to make four quarter-square triangles.
    - Yield: 4 triangles

Medium
- Cut one 3 1/2" square.

Dark
- Cut four 2 3/8" squares.
  - Cut the squares once, diagonally, to make two half-square triangles from each.
    - Yield: 8 triangles

Sew two half-square triangles to each quarter-square triangle, pressing the first seam before sewing the second, to make four units like the one at the left. Arrange the pieced units and remaining squares to make a Sawtooth Star block. Complete the block as directed for the Nine Patch block.

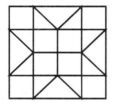 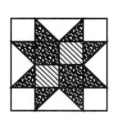

Indian Star

Light
- Cut four 2" squares.
- Cut one 4 1/4" square.
  - Cut the 4 1/4" square twice, diagonally, to make four quarter-square triangles.
    - Yield: 4 triangles

Medium
- Cut two 2" squares.

Dark
- Cut two 2" squares.
- Cut four 2 3/8" squares.
  - Cut the 2 3/8" squares once, diagonally, to make two half-square triangles from each.
    - Yield: 8 triangles

Use the 2" squares of medium and dark fabrics to piece a four patch unit. Refer to the Double Four Patch block for more instruction. Complete the block as directed for the Sawtooth Star block, using the four patch unit in place of the large square.

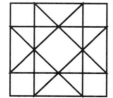 

Evening Star

Light
- Cut four 2" squares.
- Cut two 2 3/8" squares.
  - Cut the 2 3/8" squares once, diagonally, to make two half-square triangles from each.
    - Yield: 4 triangles
- Cut one 4 1/4" square.
  - Cut the 4 1/4" square twice, diagonally, to make four quarter-square triangles.
    - Yield: 4 triangles

Dark
Cut one 2 5/8" square.
Cut four 2 3/8" squares.
Cut the 2 3/8" squares once, diagonally, to make two half-square triangles from each.
Yield: 8 triangles

Sew a small half-square triangle of light fabric to each side of the 2 5/8" square of dark fabric to make a unit like the one shown at the left. Complete the block as directed for the Sawtooth Star block, using the unit at the left in place of the large center square.

Dutchman's Puzzle #1

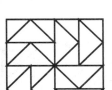 

Light
Cut eight 2 3/8" squares.
Cut the squares once, diagonally, to make two half-square triangles from each.
Yield: 16 triangles

Medium
Cut one 4 1/4" square.
Cut the square twice, diagonally, to make four quarter-square triangles.
Yield: 4 triangles

Dark
Cut one 4 1/4" square.
Cut the square twice, diagonally, to make four quarter-square triangles.
Yield: 4 triangles

Sew two half-square triangles to each quarter-square triangle, pressing the first seam before doing the second one, to make four of each unit like those at the far left. Sew the pieced units into pairs. Arrange the four quarters to make a Dutchman's Puzzle #1 block. Complete the block as directed for the Pinwheel #1 block.

King's Crown

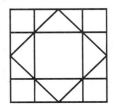 

Light
Cut four 2 3/8" squares.
Cut the squares once, diagonally, to make two half-square triangles from each.
Yield: 8 triangles

Medium
Cut four 2" squares.
Cut one 3 1/2" square.

Dark
Cut one 4 1/4" square.
Cut the square twice, diagonally, to make four quarter-square triangles.
Yield: 4 triangles

Use the triangles to piece four units as shown at the left. Press. Arrange these units with the squares to make a King's Crown block. Complete the block as directed for the Nine Patch block.

67

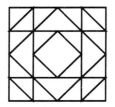 

Hourglass

Light
    Cut one 2 5/8" square.
    Cut six 2 3/8" squares.
        Cut the 2 3/8" squares once, diagonally, to make two half-square triangles from each.
                Yield: 12 triangles

Medium
    Cut four 2 3/8" squares.
        Cut the squares once, diagonally, to make two half-square triangles from each.
                Yield: 8 triangles

Dark
    Cut one 4 1/4" square.
        Cut the square twice, diagonally, to make four quarter-square triangles.
                Yield: 4 triangles

 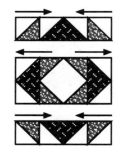

Use the four quarter-square triangles and eight of the light half-square triangles to piece four units like the one at the far left. Press. Make four half-square triangle units with four light and four medium triangles. Press.

Sew the remaining four triangles of medium fabric to the sides of the center square, pressing the seam allowances toward the triangle after sewing it on. Arrange the pieced units to make an Hourglass block. Complete the block, as directed for the Nine Patch block, but refer to the arrows for pressing directions.

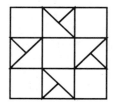 

Spinning Star #1

Light
    Cut four 2 1/2" squares.
    Cut one 3 1/4" square.
        Cut the 3 1/4" square twice, diagonally, to make four quarter-square triangles.
                Yield: 4 triangles

Medium
    Cut two 2 7/8" squares.
        Cut the squares once, diagonally, to make two half-square triangles from each.
                Yield: 4 triangles

Dark
    Cut one 2 1/2" square.
    Cut one 3 1/4" square.
        Cut the 3 1/4" square twice, diagonally, to make four quarter-square triangles.
                Yield: 4 triangles

Piece four units like the one shown at the left. Refer to the Double Pinwheel block for more instruction. Arrange the pieced units and squares to make a Spinning Star #1 block. Complete the block as directed for the Nine Patch block.

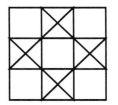 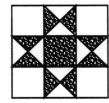

Ohio Star

Light
   Cut four 2 1/2" squares.
   Cut two 3 1/4" squares.
      Cut the 3 1/4" squares twice, diagonally, to make four quarter-square triangles from each.
                          Yield: 8 triangles

Dark
   Cut one 2 1/2" square.
   Cut two 3 1/4" squares.
      Cut the 3 1/4" squares twice, diagonally, to make four quarter-square triangles from each.
                          Yield: 8 triangles

Piece four units like the one shown at the left. Refer to the Big Dipper block for more instruction. Arrange the pieced units and squares to make an Ohio Star block. Complete the block as directed for the Nine Patch block.

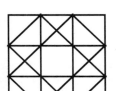 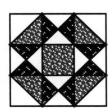

Swamp Angel

Light
   Cut two 2 7/8" squares.
      Cut the 2 7/8" squares once, diagonally, to make two half-square triangles from each.
                          Yield: 4 triangles

   Cut two 3 1/4" squares.
      Cut the 3 1/4" squares twice, diagonally, to make four quarter-square triangles from each.
                          Yield: 8 triangles

Medium
   Cut one 2 1/2" square.
   Cut two 2 7/8" squares.
      Cut the 2 7/8" squares once, diagonally, to make two half-square triangles from each.
                          Yield: 4 triangles

Dark
   Cut two 3 1/4" squares.
      Cut the squares twice, diagonally, to make four quarter-square triangles from each.
                          Yield: 8 triangles

Use the half-square triangles to piece four half-square triangle units. Press. Piece four units like the one at the left, using the quarter-square triangles. Refer to the Big Dipper block for more instruction. Arrange the pieced units and square to make a Swamp Angel block. Complete the block as directed for the Nine Patch block.

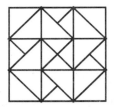 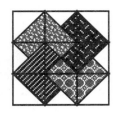

Card Trick

Light
    Cut two 2 7/8" squares.
        Cut the 2 7/8" squares once, diagonally, to make two half-square triangles from each.
            Yield: 4 triangles
    Cut one 3 1/4" square.
        Cut the 3 1/4" square twice, diagonally, to make four quarter-square triangles.
            Yield: 4 triangles

Darks - *Use four fabrics and cut the following pieces from each.*
    Cut one 2 7/8" square.
        Cut the 2 7/8" square once, diagonally, to make two half-square triangles.
            Yield: 2 triangles

    Cut one 3 1/4" square.
        Cut the 3 1/4" square twice, diagonally, to make four quarter-square triangles.
            Yield: 4 triangles

Arrange the pieces to make a Card Trick block. Label and save the extra triangles for future blocks. Piece four corner units. Sew the remaining triangles into units like those at the left, paying close attention to your fabric placement. Refer to the Double Pinwheel block for more instruction. Arrange the pieced units and squares to make a Card Trick block. Complete the block as directed for the Nine Patch block.

London Roads

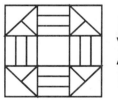 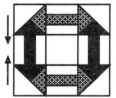

Light
    Cut one 2 1/2" square.
    Cut eight 1 1/8" x 2 1/2" rectangles.
    Cut two 2 7/8" squares.
        Cut the 2 7/8" squares once, diagonally, to make two half-square triangles from each.
            Yield: 4 triangles

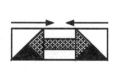

Medium
    Cut two 1 1/4" x 2 1/2" rectangles.
    Cut one 3 1/4" square.
        Cut the square twice, diagonally, to make four quarter-square triangles.
            Yield: 4 triangles

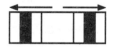

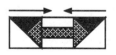

Dark
    Cut two 1 1/4" x 2 1/2" rectangles.
    Cut one 3 1/4" square.
        Cut the square twice, diagonally, to make four quarter-square triangles.
            Yield: 4 triangles

Use the pieces to make two of each unit shown at the left. Refer to the Double Pinwheel block for more instruction. Sew a light rectangle to each long side of the other four rectangles. Press. Arrange the pieced units and square to make a London Roads block. Complete the block as directed for the Nine Patch block, but refer to the arrows for pressing directions.

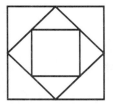 

Economy

Light
- Cut one 4 1/4" square.
  - Cut the square twice, diagonally, to make four quarter-square triangles.
              Yield: 4 triangles

Medium
- Cut one 3 1/2" square.

Dark
- Cut two 3 7/8" squares.
  - Cut the squares once, diagonally, to make two half-square triangles from each.
              Yield: 4 triangles

Sew a quarter-square triangle to each side of the square, pressing the seam allowances toward the triangle after each is added. Add the half-square triangles to complete the block. Press the seam allowances toward the triangles after each is added.

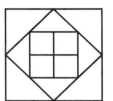 

Snail's Trail

Light
- Cut two 2" squares.
- Cut one 3 7/8" square.
  - Cut the 3 7/8" square once, diagonally, to make two half-square triangles.
              Yield: 2 triangles
- Cut one 4 1/4" square.
  - Cut the 4 1/4" square twice, diagonally, to make four quarter-square triangles.
              Yield: 4 triangles

Dark
- Same as light.

Use the squares to piece a four patch unit for the block's center. Refer to the Double Four Patch block for more instruction. Arrange the four patch unit and triangles to make a Snail's Trail block. Label and save the leftover quarter-square triangles for future use. Complete the block as directed for the Economy block, being careful to place the dark and light triangles correctly.

71

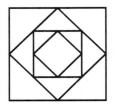 

Twelve Triangles

Light
    Cut one 2 5/8" square.
    Cut one 4 1/4" square.
        Cut the 4 1/4" square twice, diagonally, to make
        four quarter-square triangles.
                                  Yield: 4 triangles

Medium
    Cut two 2 3/8" squares.
        Cut the squares once, diagonally, to make two
        half-square triangles from each.
                                  Yield: 4 triangles

Dark
    Cut two 3 7/8" squares.
        Cut the squares once, diagonally, to make two
        half-square triangles from each.
                                  Yield: 4 triangles

Construct this block as directed for the Economy block. Begin by adding the smallest triangles to the square first.

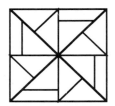 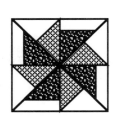

Old Fashioned Pinwheel

Light
    Cut four 1 3/8" x 3 7/8" rectangles.
    Cut one 4 1/4" square.
        Cut the square twice, diagonally, to make four
        quarter-square triangles.
                                  Yield: 4 triangles

Medium
    Cut one 4 1/4" square.
        Cut the square twice, diagonally, to make four
        quarter-square triangles.
                                  Yield: 4 triangles

Dark
    Cut two 3" squares.
        Cut the squares once, diagonally, to make two
        half-square triangles from each.
                                  Yield: 4 triangles

 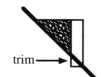

Sew a rectangle to each of the half-square triangles of dark fabric. Press. Trim the excess of the rectangle as shown.

Sew the quarter-square triangles into four pairs. Press. Sew the units from above to these triangle pairs. Press.

Complete the block as directed for the Pinwheel #1 block.

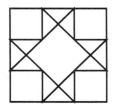 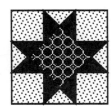

Aunt Eliza's Star

Light
    Cut four 2 1/2" squares.
    Cut one 3 1/4" square.
        Cut the 3 1/4" square twice, diagonally, to make four quarter-square triangles.
        Yield: 4 triangles

Medium
    Cut one 3 3/8" square.

Dark
    Cut two 3 1/4" squares.
        Cut the squares twice, diagonally, to make four quarter-square triangles from each.
        Yield: 8 triangles

Make two units like the one above at the near left. Press. Sew these to two opposite sides of the large square of medium fabric. Press.

Sew the remaining quarter-square triangles into pairs, making two of each. Press. Sew these to the remaining 2 1/2" squares to make two sections, as shown in the bottom sketch. Press. You now have three diagonal rows. Sew them together and press the seam allowances toward the middle row.

Country Farm

Light
    Cut four 2 1/2" squares.
    Cut one 3 1/4" square.
        Cut the 3 1/4" square twice, diagonally, to make four quarter-square triangles.
        Yield: 4 triangles

Medium
    Cut one 2 7/8" square.
        Cut the square once, diagonally, to make two half-square triangles.
        Yield: 2 triangles

Dark
    Cut one 2 7/8" square.
        Cut the 2 7/8" square once, diagonally, to make two half-square triangles.
        Yield: 2 triangles
    Cut two 3 1/4" squares.
        Cut the 3 1/4" squares twice, diagonally, to make four quarter-square triangles from each.
        Yield: 8 triangles

Use the half-square triangles of medium and dark fabric to make a unit like the one at the left. Refer to the Big Dipper block for more instruction. Complete the block as directed for the Aunt Eliza's Star block, using the pieced unit in place of the large center square.

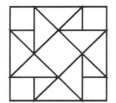 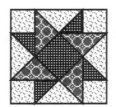

Spinning Star #2

Light
    Cut four 2" squares.
    Cut one 4 1/4" square.
        Cut the 4 1/4" square twice, diagonally, to make four quarter-square triangles.
        Yield: 4 triangles

Medium
    Cut one 4 1/4" square.
        Cut the square twice, diagonally, to make four quarter-square triangles.
        Yield: 4 triangles

Dark
    Cut one 2 5/8" square.
    Cut two 2 3/8" squares.
        Cut the 2 3/8" squares once, diagonally, to make two half-square triangles from each.
        Yield: 4 triangles

Follow the two sketches to make four units like the one at the near left.

Arrange the pieced units with the remaining triangles and square to make the Spinning Star #2 block. Sew the pieces into three diagonal rows. Press. Complete the block, referring to the Aunt Eliza's Star block for more instruction, if necessary.

Snowball

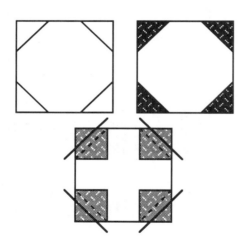

The remaining twenty blocks require the sew & flip technique. Detailed instructions are on page 9.

Light
    Cut one 6 1/2" square.

Dark
    Cut four 2 1/2" squares.

Place a square of dark fabric, RST, on each corner of the large light square. Stitch, as shown by the dotted lines. Trim, as shown by the solid lines. Press the seam allowances toward the dark fabric.

Bow Tie

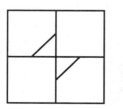 

Light
    Cut two 3 1/2" squares.

Dark
    Cut two 3 1/2" squares.
    Cut two 2" squares.

Place a small square of dark fabric on one corner of each large square of light fabric. Stitch, as shown by the dotted line, and trim, as shown by the solid line. Press. Complete the block as directed for the Double Four Patch block.

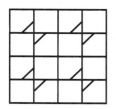 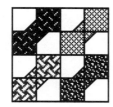

Bow Ties #1

Light
 Cut eight 2" squares.

Dark - *Use four different fabrics. Cut the following from each.*
 Cut two 2" squares.
 Cut two 1 1/4" squares.

Make four small bow ties as directed on the previous page. Arrange the ties to make a Bow Ties #1 block. Complete the block as directed for the Pinwheel #1 block.

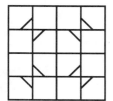 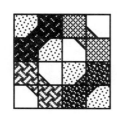

Bow Ties #2

Light - *Use two different fabrics. Cut the following from each.*
 Cut four 2" squares.

Dark - *Use four different fabrics. Cut the following from each.*
 Cut two 2" squares.
 Cut two 1 1/4" squares.

Pair the dark and light fabrics so that each of the small bow tie units contains only two fabrics. Make four small bow ties as directed on page 74. Arrange the ties to make a Bow Ties #2 block. Complete the block as directed for the Pinwheel #1 block.

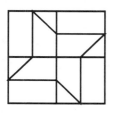 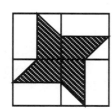

Twinkle Toes

Light
 Cut four 2" x 3 1/2" rectangles.
 Cut four 2" squares.

Dark
 Cut four 2" x 3 1/2" rectangles.

Place a square of light fabric, RST, on one end of each dark rectangle. Stitch on the diagonal *in the direction shown by the dotted line*. Trim and press the seam allowances toward the dark fabric. Sew each unit to a light rectangle. Press. Complete the block as directed for the Pinwheel #1 block.

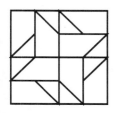 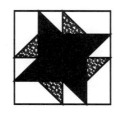

Pas de Deux

Light
 Cut four 2" x 3 1/2" rectangles.
 Cut four 2" squares.

Medium
 Cut four 2" squares.

Dark
 Cut four 2" x 3 1/2" rectangles.

Place a light square of fabric, RST, on one end of each dark rectangle. Stitch on the diagonal *in the direction shown by the dotted line*. Trim and press the seam allowances toward the dark. Repeat with the medium squares and light rectangles, stitching in the direction shown. This is the reverse of the first four units. Sew these units into pairs. Press. Complete the block as directed for the Pinwheel #1 block.

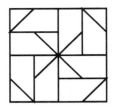 

Paddle Wheel

Light
    Cut four 2" x 3 1/2" rectangles.
    Cut four 2" squares.

Medium
    Cut four 2" squares.

Dark
    Cut four 2" x 3 1/2" rectangles.

Complete the block as directed on the previous page for the Pas de Deux block, except arrange the four quarters of the block, as shown at the left.

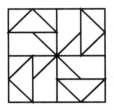 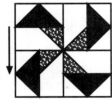

Dutchman's Puzzle #2

Light
    Cut four 2" x 3 1/2" rectangles.
    Cut four 2 3/8" squares.
        Cut the squares once, diagonally, to make two half-square triangles from each.
                    Yield: 8 triangles

Medium
    Cut four 2" squares.

Dark
    Cut one 4 1/4" square.
        Cut the square twice, diagonally, to make four quarter-square triangles.
                    Yield: 4 triangles

Use all of the triangles to make four units like the one at the left. Refer to the Sawtooth Star block for more instruction.

Place a square of medium fabric on the end of each light rectangle. Stitch on the diagonal, making sure to sew in the direction shown by the dotted line. Trim and press the seam allowances toward the medium fabric. Arrange the pieced sections to make four units like the one directly at the left. Press.

Arrange the units to make a Dutchman's Puzzle #2 block. Complete the block as directed for the Pinwheel #1 block, but refer to the arrows for pressing directions.

76

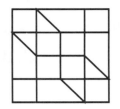 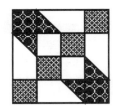

Road to Oklahoma

Light
   Cut four 2" x 3 1/2" rectangles.
   Cut two 2" squares.

Medium
   Cut four 2" squares.

Dark
   Cut six 2" squares.

Use two light and two medium 2" squares to make a four patch unit for the center of the block.

Use the four light rectangles and four of the dark 2" squares to make two of each of the units like those at the left. Refer to the Twinkle Toes block for more instruction. Arrange the pieced sections and remaining squares to make a Road to Oklahoma block. Complete the block as directed for the Nine Patch block.

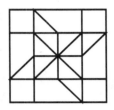 

Jackson's Star

Light
   Cut four 2" x 3 1/2" rectangles.

Medium
   Cut four 2" squares.
   Cut two 2 3/8" squares.
      Cut the 2 3/8" squares once, diagonally, to make two half-square triangles from each.
                     Yield: 4 triangles

Dark
   Cut four 2" squares.
   Cut two 2 3/8" squares.
      Cut the 2 3/8" squares once, diagonally, to make two half-square triangles from each.
                     Yield: 4 triangles

Use all of the triangles to make four half-square triangle units. Press. Arrange these units to make the pinwheel for the center of the block. Refer to the Pinwheel #1 block for more instruction.

Make four units like the one at the left. Refer to the Dutchman's Puzzle #2 block for more instruction. Arrange the pieced units and remaining squares to make a Jackson's Star block. Complete the block as directed for the Nine Patch block.

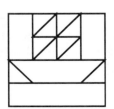 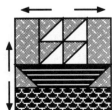

Ship

Light
   Cut two 2 3/8" squares.
      Cut the squares once, diagonally, to make two half-square triangles from each.
                     Yield: 4 triangles

Medium
   Cut two 2" squares.
   Cut two 2" x 3 1/2" rectangles.

Medium (continued)
Cut two 2 3/8" squares.
Cut the 2 3/8" squares once, diagonally, to make two half-square triangles from each.
Yield: 4 triangles

Dark #1
Cut one 2" x 6 1/2" rectangle.

Dark #2
Cut one 2" x 6 1/2" rectangle.

Use all of the triangles to make four half-square triangle units. Press. Arrange these units to make the sails of the ship. Sew them together as you would a four patch and press. Add a 2" x 3 1/2" rectangle to each side of the sail section. Press.

Make the boat section by placing a 2" square of medium fabric, RST, on each end of the dark #1 fabric. Stitch as shown by the dotted lines. Trim and press the seam allowances toward the boat. Sew the three rows together to complete the Ship block. Press.

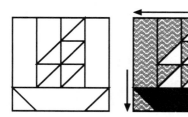

Tall Ship

Light
Cut one 2" square.
Cut two 2 3/8" squares.
Cut the 2 3/8" squares once, diagonally, to make two half-square triangles from each.
Yield: 4 triangles

Medium
Cut two 2" x 5" rectangles.
Cut one 2" x 3 1/2" rectangle.
Cut two 2" squares.
Cut two 2 3/8" squares.
Cut the 2 3/8" squares once, diagonally, to make two half-square triangles from each.
Yield: 4 triangles

Dark
Cut one 2" x 6 1/2" rectangle.

Make the boat section as directed for the Ship block above, using the dark rectangle and two 2" squares of medium.

Use the triangles to piece four half-square triangle units. Press.

Use the 2" x 3 1/2" rectangle of medium fabric and the 2" square of light fabric to make one unit like the one at the left. Refer to the Dutchman's Puzzle #2 block for more instruction.

Arrange all of the units to make a Tall Ship block. Make the sail section by piecing four vertical rows. Sew the rows together. Press. Add the boat to the bottom of the block. Press.

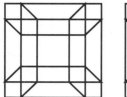

Rabbit's Paw

Light
   Cut four 1 1/2" x 4 1/2" rectangles.
   Cut four 1 1/2" squares.

Medium
   Cut four 1 1/2" x 2 1/2" rectangles.

Dark #1
   Cut one 2 1/2" square.
   Cut four 1 1/2" squares.

Dark #2
   Cut eight 1 1/2" squares.

Use the four light rectangles and eight dark #2 squares to make four units like the one at the left. Refer to the Ship block for more instruction. Piece a Puss in the Corner unit with the squares of dark #1 and medium rectangles for the center of the block. Refer to the Puss in the Corner #1 block for more instruction. Arrange the pieced sections and remaining squares of light fabric to make the Rabbit's Paw block. Complete the block as directed for the Nine Patch block.

North Country

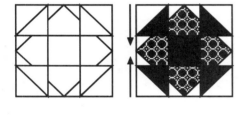

Light
   Cut eight 1 1/2" squares.
   Cut two 2 7/8" squares.
     Cut the 2 7/8" squares once, diagonally, to make two half-square triangles from each.
          Yield: 4 triangles

Medium
   Cut four 2 1/2" squares.

Dark
   Cut one 2 1/2" square.
   Cut two 2 7/8" squares.
     Cut the 2 7/8" squares once, diagonally, to make two half-square triangles from each.
          Yield: 4 triangles

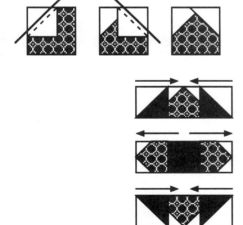

With the sew & flip technique, using the four medium squares and eight light squares, make four units as shown above at the left. After sewing on the first square, it must be trimmed and pressed prior to adding the second one. Use the triangles to make four half-square triangle units. Press. Arrange the pieced units and center square to make a North Country block. Complete the block as directed for the Nine Patch block, but refer to the arrows for pressing directions.

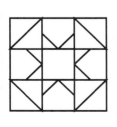 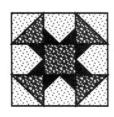

Jake's Star

Light
   Cut four 2 1/2" squares.
   Cut two 2 7/8" squares.
     Cut the 2 7/8" squares once, diagonally, to make two half-square triangles from each.
          Yield: 4 triangles

Medium
    Cut one 2 1/2" square.
    Cut two 2 7/8" squares.
        Cut the 2 7/8" squares once, diagonally, to make two half-square triangles from each.
                Yield: 4 triangles

Dark
    Cut eight 1 1/2" squares.

 Use the four 2 1/2" squares of light and eight squares of dark to make four units like the one at the left. Refer to the North Country block for more instruction.

Complete this block exactly like the North Country block, except rotate the four units from above to make the block look like the Jake's Star block.

Quilter's Dream

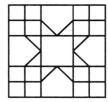 

Light
    Cut eight 1 1/2" squares.
    Cut four 2 1/2" squares.

Medium
    Cut eight 1 1/2" squares.
    Cut one 2 1/2" square.

Dark
    Cut eight 1 1/2" squares.

Use the 1 1/2" squares of light and medium fabrics to make four four patch units. Refer to the Double Four Patch block for more instruction. Complete the block as directed for Jake's Star, substituting the four patch units for the half-square triangle units.

Capital T's

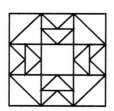 

Light
    Cut one 2 1/2" square.
    Cut two 2 7/8" squares.
        Cut the 2 7/8" squares once, diagonally, to make two half-square triangles from each.
                Yield: 4 triangles
    Cut two 3 1/4" squares.
        Cut the 3 1/4" squares twice, diagonally, to make four quarter-square triangles from each.
                Yield: 8 triangles

Darks - *Use four fabrics and cut the following from each.*
    Cut two 1 7/8" squares.
        Cut the 1 7/8" squares once, diagonally, to make two half-square triangles from each.
                Yield: 4 triangles
    Cut one 2 7/8" square.
        Cut the 2 7/8" square once, diagonally, to make two half-square triangles.
                Yield: 2 triangles

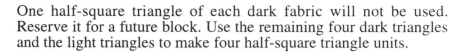

One half-square triangle of each dark fabric will not be used. Reserve it for a future block. Use the remaining four dark triangles and the light triangles to make four half-square triangle units.

Arrange all of the triangles and half-square units from above to make the Capital T's block. Sew the small half-square triangles to the quarter-square triangles to make two of each unit like those in the top row at the left. Press after you add each triangle. Pay close attention to where the triangles go in order to achieve your block pattern. Sew the like units into pairs. Press. Complete the block as directed for the Nine Patch block.

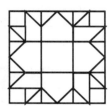

Weathervane

Light
    Cut sixteen 1 1/2" squares.
    Cut two 1 7/8" squares.
        Cut the 1 7/8" squares once, diagonally, to make
        two half-square triangles from each.
                Yield: 4 triangles

Medium
    Cut four 2 1/2" squares.

Dark
    Cut four 1 1/2" x 2 1/2" rectangles.
    Cut one 2 1/2" square.
    Cut two 1 7/8" squares.
        Cut the squares once, diagonally, to make two
        half-square triangles from each.
                Yield: 4 triangles

Use the four squares of medium and eight of the squares of light to make four units like the one at the left. Refer to the North Country block for more instruction.

Use the triangles to piece four half-square triangle units. Press. Add a 1 1/2" square of light to each. Press.

Use the four dark rectangles, four light squares, and the sew & flip technique to make four units like the one shown directly at the left. Be sure to piece them exactly as shown! Refer to the Twinkle Toes block for more instruction. Sew these to the pieced sections that you just completed above. Press. Arrange all of the pieced sections and the remaining square to make a Weathervane block. Complete the block as directed for the Nine Patch block.

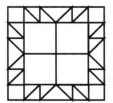

Paw Prints

Light
    Cut four 1 1/2" squares.
    Cut four 1 7/8" squares.
        Cut the 1 7/8" squares once, diagonally, to make
        two half-square triangles from each.
                Yield: 8 triangles
    Cut one 3 1/4" square.
        Cut the 3 1/4" square twice, diagonally, to make
        four quarter-square triangles.
                Yield: 4 triangles

Medium
    Cut two 2 1/2" squares.
    Cut four 1 7/8" squares.
        Cut the 1 7/8" squares once, diagonally, to make
        two half-square triangles from each.
                                  Yield: 8 triangles

Dark
    Cut two 2 1/2" squares.
    Cut four 1 7/8" squares.
        Cut the 1 7/8" squares once, diagonally, to make
        two half-square triangles from each.
                                  Yield: 8 triangles

Use four dark, four medium, and eight light half-square triangles to make four half-square triangle units like each one shown at the left. Press.

Use the remaining triangles to piece two of each of the units shown directly at the left. Press the seam allowances away from the light triangles.

Arrange all of the pieced units from above to make two of each section shown in the bottom sketch. Press. Piece the four patch section for the center of the block. Refer to the Double Four Patch block for more instruction. Arrange all of your pieces to make a Paw Prints block. Complete the block as directed for the Nine Patch block.

Oh, My Stars!

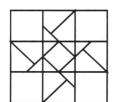 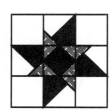

Light
    Cut four 2 1/2" squares.
    Cut two 2 7/8" squares.
        Cut the 2 7/8" squares once, diagonally, to make
        two half-square triangles from each.
                                  Yield: 4 triangles

Medium
    Cut eight 1 1/2" squares.

Dark
    Cut one 2 1/2" square.
    Cut two 2 7/8" squares.
        Cut the 2 7/8" squares once, diagonally, to make
        two half-square triangles from each.
                                  Yield: 4 triangles

Use the half-square triangles to piece four half-square triangle units. Press. Place a square of medium fabric, RST, on each unit, as shown. Stitch, check your work to make sure it looks exactly like the sketch. Trim and press the seam allowances toward the medium fabric.

Use the square of dark, four squares of medium, and the sew & flip method to make a section like the one at the left. Press the seam allowances toward the medium fabric piece as each is added.

Arrange the pieced sections with the light squares to make the Oh, My Stars block. Complete the block as directed for the Nine Patch block.

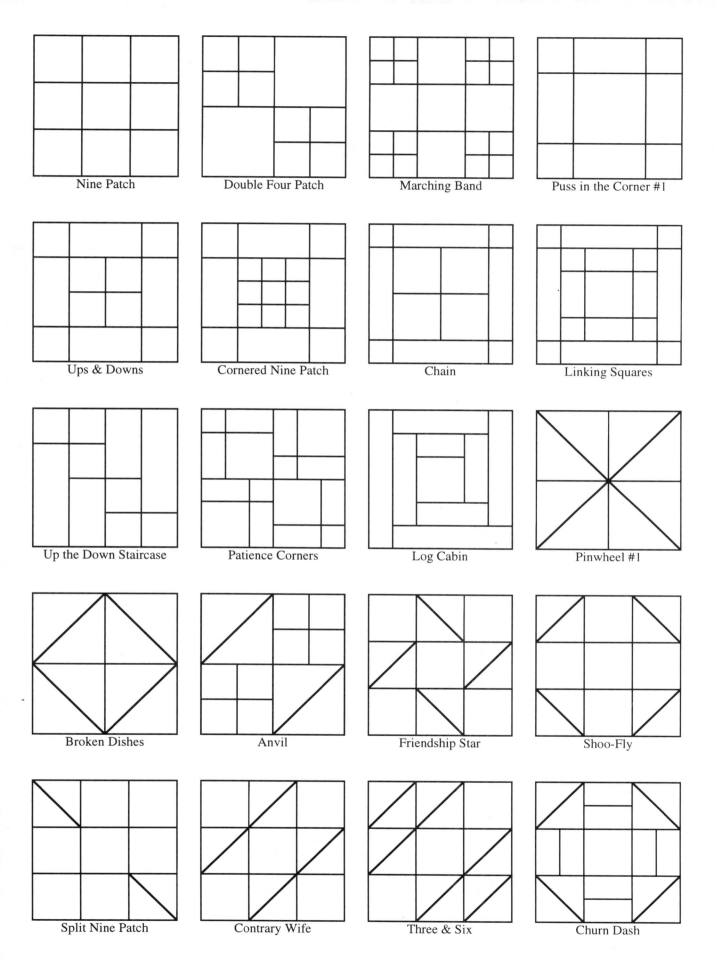

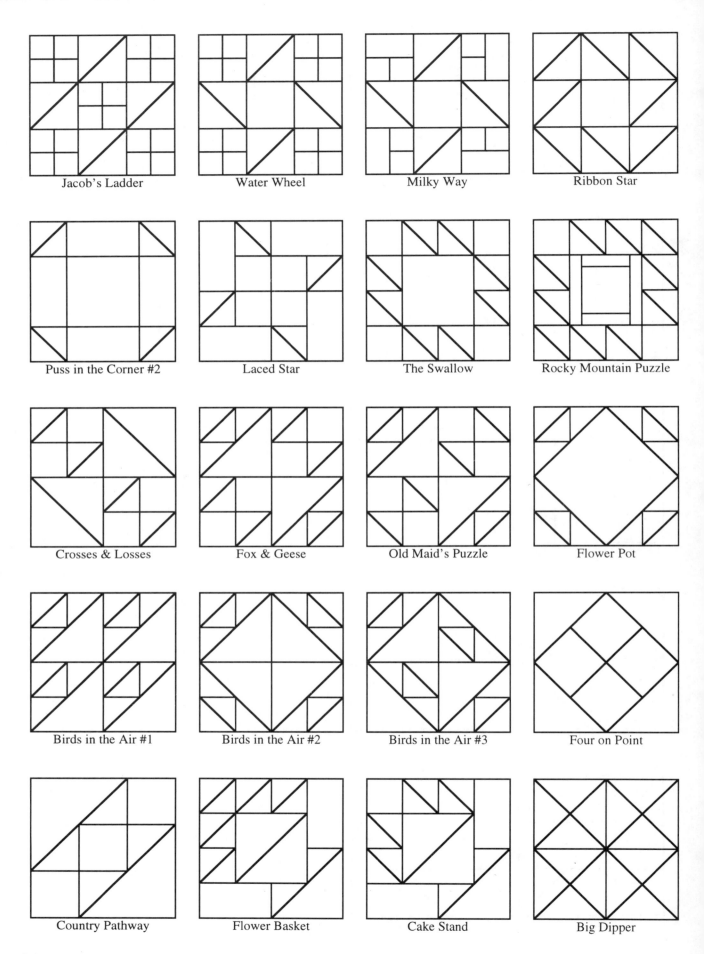

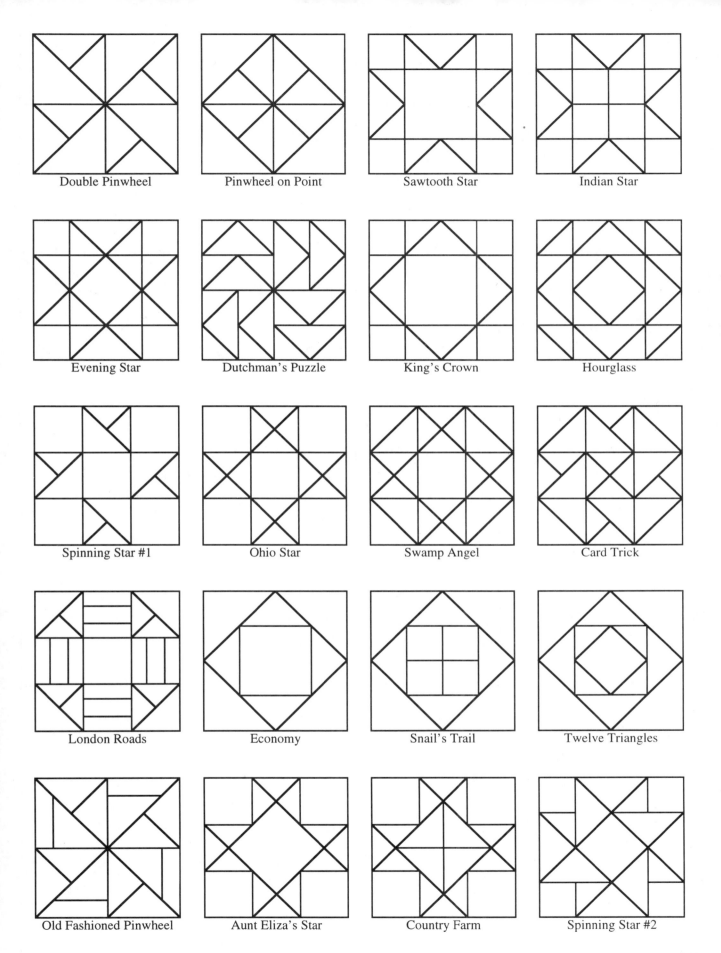

85

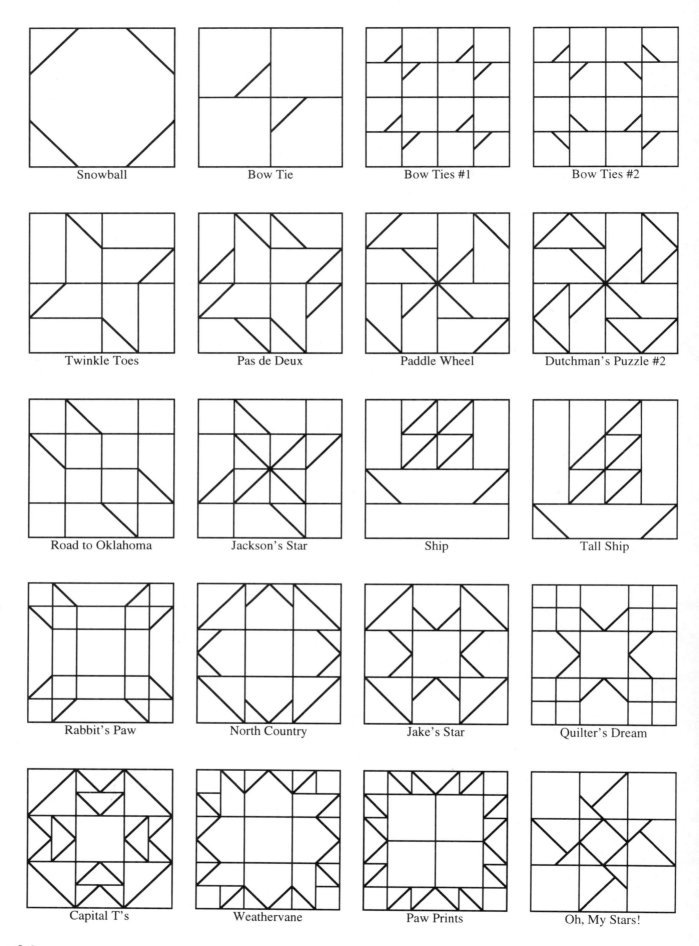

Index

Anvil 54, 83
Aunt Eliza's Star 73, 85

Big Dipper 65, 84
Birds in the Air #1 62, 84
Birds in the Air #2 62, 84
Birds in the Air #3 63, 84
Bow Tie 74, 86
Bow Ties #1 75, 86
Bow Ties #2 75, 86
Broken Dishes 54, 83

Cake Stand 64, 84
Capital T's 80, 86
Card Trick 70, 85
Chain 52, 83
Churn Dash 56, 83
Contrary Wife 55, 83
Cornered Nine Patch 51, 83
Country Farm 73, 85
Country Pathway 63, 84
Crosses & Losses 60, 84

Double Four Patch 50, 83
Double Pinwheel 65, 85
Dutchman's Puzzle #1 67, 85
Dutchman's Puzzle #2 76, 86

Economy 71, 85
Evening Star 66, 85

Flower Basket 64, 84
Flower Pot 62, 84
Four on Point 63, 84
Fox & Geese 61, 84
Friendship Star 54, 83

Hourglass 68, 85

Indian Star 66, 85

Jackson's Star 77, 86
Jacob's Ladder 57, 84
Jake's Star 79, 86

King's Crown 67, 85

Laced Star 59, 84
Linking Squares 52, 83
Log Cabin 53, 83
London Roads 70, 85

Marching Band 51, 83
Milky Way 57, 84

Nine Patch 50, 83
North Country 79, 86

Oh, My Stars! 82, 86
Ohio Star 69, 85
Old Fashioned Pinwheel 72, 85
Old Maid's Puzzle 61, 84

Paddle Wheel 76, 86
Pas de Deux 75, 86
Patience Corners 53, 83
Paw Prints 81, 86
Pinwheel #1 53, 83
Pinwheel on Point 65, 85
Puss in the Corner #1 51, 83
Puss in the Corner #2 58, 84

Quilter's Dream 80, 86

Rabbit's Paw 79, 86
Ribbon Star 58, 84
Road to Oklahoma 77, 86
Rocky Mountain Puzzle 60, 84

Sawtooth Star 66, 85
Ship 77, 86
Shoo-Fly 55, 83
Snail's Trail 71, 85
Snowball 74, 86
Spinning Star #1 68, 85
Spinning Star #2 74, 85
Split Nine Patch 55, 83
Swallow, The 59, 84
Swamp Angel 69, 85

Tall Ship 78, 86
Three & Six 56, 83
Twelve Triangles 72, 85
Twinkle Toes 75, 86

Up the Down Staircase 52, 83
Ups & Downs 51, 83

Water Wheel 57, 84
Weathervane 81, 86

Conversion Charts

Use these charts to convert the cutting measurements to make 12" blocks.

Squares

if, for 6" blocks, you cut	then, for 12" blocks, cut
1 1/4"	2"
1 1/2"	2 1/2"
2"	3 1/2"
2 1/2"	4 1/2"
2 5/8"	4 3/4"
3 3/8"	6 1/8"
3 1/2"	6 1/2"
4 3/4"	9"
6 1/2"	12 1/2"

Rectangles

if, for 6" blocks, you cut	then, for 12" blocks, cut
1" x 2 1/2"	1 1/2" x 4 1/2"
1" x 3 1/2"	1 1/2" x 6 1/2"
1 1/8" x 2 1/2"	1 3/4" x 4 1/2"
1 1/4" x 2 1/2"	2" x 4 1/2"
1 3/8" x 3 7/8"	2 1/4" x 6 7/8"
1 1/2" x 2 1/2"	2 1/2" x 4 1/2"
1 1/2" x 3 1/2"	2 1/2" x 6 1/2"
1 1/2" x 4 1/2"	2 1/2" x 8 1/2"
1 1/2" x 5 1/2"	2 1/2" x 10 1/2"
1 1/2" x 6 1/2"	2 1/2" x 12 1/2"
2" x 3 1/2"	3 1/2" x 6 1/2"
2" x 5"	3 1/2" x 9 1/2"
2" x 6 1/2"	3 1/2" x 12 1/2"

Half-Square Triangles

if, for 6" blocks, you cut squares	then, for 12" blocks, cut squares
1 7/8"	2 7/8"
2 3/8"	3 7/8"
2 7/8"	4 7/8"
3"	5 1/8"
3 7/8"	6 7/8"
4 7/8"	8 7/8"

Quarter-Square Triangles

if, for 6" blocks, you cut squares	then, for 12" blocks, cut squares
3 1/4"	5 1/4"
4 1/4"	7 1/4"